*Jesus
and the Hunger
for Things Unknown*

Pierre Talec

Jesus
and the Hunger
for Things Unknown

translated from the French by
Joachim Neugroschel

The Seabury Press / New York

1982
The Seabury Press
815 Second Avenue
New York, N.Y. 10017

Originally published in one volume
as *Les Choses de la Foi: Croire à l'essentiel.*
Copyright © 1973 Éditions du Centurion, Paris.
This is the first of two volumes.

Printed in the United States of America

Library of Congress Cataloging in Publication Data
Talec, Pierre.
    Jesus and the hunger for things unknown.
Translation of: Les choses de la foi.
1. Jesus Christ—Person and offices. 2. Christian
life—Catholic authors. I. Title.
BT202.T3713   248.4'82   82–3255
ISBN 0–8164–0510–7

*To my mother, to my father,
the roots of my faith.*

*Peut-être que j'ai faim de choses inconnues.
Perhaps I hunger for things unknown.*
VALÉRY LARBAUD

Contents

The Foretaste of God

Live! Live for the joy of it. Don't just exist. Life races by. Don't just try to get it over with like a necessary task or chore. Life is short. Go far into yourself and find out everything you can. Don't live for the weekend. Store every today in your private granary. Live for others, but don't delude yourself with self-righteousness. Live for yourself, too; because, in the flow of love towards the Other, if you lose track of yourself, you are deceiving yourself. Love yourself the way God loves you. Be alive. Truly alive. Celebrate the goodness of life.

Live in broad daylight! Develop a taste for life. What do you think of the light of the world? What do you think of the salt of the earth? The Gospels have nothing to do with indirect lighting. You don't light a candle to put it under a bushel; you place it in a candlestick. There, it burns for all the people in the house. But don't feel you have to shine in the eyes of the world. Illuminate your inner self. Don't look for light on high peaks. Our God is not the God of Olympus. Jesus is the ecstasy of the heart. Make sure your inner light is not really shadow. Watch where you put your salt. Don't be indifferent, don't waste your zeal, your salt. Don't live half-heartedly.

Live with fire in your soul! Slake your thirst with living water. Jesus on the cross thirsted for living water until the very last drop of his life had been spent. He who said: "Whoever drinks of this water will never thirst again" also cried: "I am thirsty!" The thirst for God is the thirst for life.

Live on love and living water! "Let me drink. Give me some of that water, so that I won't be thirsty anymore," said the woman of Samaria. Go to the source. Dig deep. The poet's words may then give you a foretaste of God, and you will say with Valéry Larbaud:

Perhaps I hunger for things unknown.

God makes us *bold* to approach him
on the road of *faith* in Christ.
Ephesians 3:12

— 1 ——————

Jesus: Someone to Recognize
Faith Is Discernment

That very same day, two of them were on their way
to a village called Emmaus, seven miles from Jerusalem,
and they were talking together about all that had happened. As they talked, Jesus himself came up and walked by
their side; but something kept them from recognizing him.
He said to them: "What were you talking about as you
walked along?" They stopped short, their faces downcast.

Then one of them, whose name was Cleopas, answered
Jesus. "You must be the only person staying in Jerusalem
who does not know the things that have been happening
there these last few days." "What things?" Jesus asked. "All
about Jesus of Nazareth," they answered, "who proved he
was a great prophet by the things he said and did in the
sight of God and of all the people; and how our chief priests
and our leaders handed him over to be sentenced to death,
and had him crucified. Our own hope has been that he
would be the one to set Israel free. And this is not all: two
whole days have gone by since it happened; and some wom-
en from our group have astounded us: they went to his
tomb in the early morning, and when they did not find his
body, they came to tell us they had seen a vision of angels
who declared he was alive. Some of our friends went to the

tomb and found everything exactly as the women had reported, they could find nothing."

Then Jesus said to them, "You foolish men! You are slow to believe the *full* message of the prophets! Was it not ordained that the Christ should suffer and so enter into his glory?" Then, starting with Moses and going through all the prophets, he explained to them the passages throughout the Scriptures that were about himself.

When they approached the village that was their destination, Jesus indicated that he intended to continue on alone, but the two men pressed him to stay with them. "It is nearly evening," they said, "and the day is almost over."

So Jesus went in to stay with them. Now while he was with them at table, he took the bread and said the blessing; then he broke it and handed it to them. And their eyes were opened and they saw who he was—but at that very instant of understanding he vanished. Then they said to each other, "Did not our hearts burn within us as he talked to us on the road and explained the Scriptures to us?".

They set out that instant and returned to Jerusalem. There they found the Eleven assembled together with their companions, who said to them, "Yes, it is true. The Lord has risen and has appeared to Simon." Then the two men told their story of what happened on the road and how they had recognized him at the breaking of bread.

(Luke 24: 13–35)

Take Life as It Comes

The road of faith is the road of life. The road of life on earth is the road of eternal life. Eternal life is not something, it is Someone: the Risen Christ. Saint Paul's famous statement "For me, living is Christ" echoes the no less famous words of Jesus: "I am the road, life. . . ." Note the apposition. Jesus doesn't say: "I am the road *of* life" but rather: "I am the road, life," and, hence, *the truth*. For the road could only be the right road. Road, Life, Truth. They're one and the same.

If you want to meet the Risen Christ, it's not enough to be on the road. Being on the road is passive. We are asked to *take* the road. And the right side of the road at that! We are asked to trake life as it comes. It comes from Christ. It goes to Christ. It is the right road, just as Christ is the right guide. In these terms, the road to Emmaus is the route of Christian faith, we must first get to know the lay of the land; we have to get the feel of the road and read the signs along the way. Don't be afraid of strolling. A road on which you can't pause to pick a blade of grass is joyless. Our goal is not to gather ideas on faith, but rather to let Christ come to us as he wishes to come. Let's not scare off the Spirit by being defensive or bitter. Like a bird, the Spirit allows us to draw near only if we approach quietly, serenely. Let our hearts fill with wonder, for Paul's words, spoken twenty centuries ago, are still true today: "God makes us bold to approach him on the Road of faith in Christ" (Ephesians 3:12). It is God himself who reveals to us that faith is an act of daring.

Going Beyond Appearances
Jesus, Near and Far

Look at those two men. They're walking. Where are they going? To Emmaus. They's don't realize they're going *to* Jesus Christ. They're going *with* Jesus Christ. They're talking about things that have happened. They must be well informed. They're coming straight from Jerusalem. They must have seen the "right" people. "He's dead. Jesus of Nazareth wasn't the One they were waiting for. No one expected this. The trial was dreadful. To think that this could happen. Crucifixion: how shameful! Whether he's a true or a false messiah, this could have been avoided! Anyway, let's not talk about it."

As though God could help communications. He *is* the Word. In that Easter dawn of the New World, the Word became flesh. New Flesh. Flesh glorified by the spiritual body of the Risen Christ. But how does Jesus make himself present? Let's not ask too many questions. Let's not start just to stop again. Let's keep walking, we'll see. For the moment, why don't we simply see what happens?

It's phenomenal. Jesus is suddenly here. He makes contact easily. He speaks gently, it seems. No grand declaration. He asks what's new. Yet he's been on the road with these two men for some time. The same old story. He passes unnoticed. People can't quite place him. "The Word was the light . . . that illuminates every man. He came into the world. He was in the world and the world did not recognize him . . ." (After John 1:9-10). And likewise, the friends going to Emmaus can't quite place him either. It's odd. People picture God differently from what he is.

What moment does he choose to reveal himself? When he appears in person, the disciples don't seem surprised. It all seems natural. Striding along, the three wayfarers fall into step, and they have the same pulse beat. God and man breathe together. In this new Genesis, the faith in Christ risen is being born. Together, they keep walking. Together, they breathe, and breathe again—inhale, exhale. The truth is, Jesus does not really have the same rhythm as they do, but he doesn't let them know it. He is light years ahead of them but he doesn't let them feel the distance. He comes close and keeps close. Faith is the intimacy, the closeness between God and man. But people take so long to see the truth! It takes the friends a long, long time to recognize him. But Jesus will be there to be recognized no matter how long it takes. All the time in the world if need be. Centuries!

Their eyes are prevented from recognizing him. Why? Not just because of the kind of camouflage that God used! Jesus appeared either as a lake fisherman or as a gardener.

They did not dare challenge the passerby on the road. They weren't bold enough to approach God the way he likes to be approached. With "fear and trembling," says the Old Testament. With *audacity*, says the New Testament. When you seek God with determination, he stops, he is there. They, however, kept on until the moment when God was at the end of his patience with seeing men who were exhausted by the search without really knowing what they were searching for. Then, Luke says, the two poor wretches on the road stopped. They marked a pause physically. But, inwardly, didn't they keep on thinking of life in terms of habits? Was this pause of theirs more than a temporary delay?

You approach God only by retreating into yourself. The men on the road to Emmaus had ideas about God. They thought they *understood*. They had decided that Jesus was indeed the Messiah who would deliver Israel. And it's no wonder they thought this; it had been repeated in synagogues for generations. They had learned their catechism well. Everyone thought the same thing. Everyone wanted it. Everyone believed in what everyone wanted. The apostles were no better than anyone else. The sons of Zebedee imagined they would have their reserved places in the Kingdom. Orchestra seats, of course—the same for all!

The disciples of Emmaus are like the wedding guests at Cana and the whole crowd who, on meeting Jesus face to face, expected him to be other than the person they saw. People always expect something other than God as he really is. God is always unexpected. And besides, there is such a vast gap between what we see and what God lets us see! Jesus came to earth not to reduce the distance between man and God, but to make it appear infinite, so that we might understand that people are called upon to grow.

Jesus first pretends to be ignorant: "What were you talking about as you came along the road?" The disciples are flabbergasted. How can anyone *not* know what's happened and what everyone would be bound to discuss? Where's he from? However, their astonishment doesn't prevent them from being cordial to him. This strange man doesn't seem to know much, and yet they allow him, an apparent ignoramus, to explain Scripture to them! Jesus then actually interprets himself to them. He goes quite far. As far as the disciples are able to go. Luke tells us that when the disciples reach the village they have originally set out for, Jesus pretends to be going further.

Jesus Pretends

It's really quite extraordinary of Saint Luke to tell us that *God pretends*. This could be taken the wrong way. People who pretend aren't very likeable. But Jesus is not playing a double game. His "pretense" is not a sham, it's a Socratic process, a method, a way of allowing people to find out by themselves something you want them to find out. Thus, Jesus lets the disciples say what they think. First, he listens. Then, when the disciples can't go any further, he helps them to understand that believing always means going beyond the point that you think you've reached. You never reach the end of Faith! Faith is an endlessly opening horizon that you strive for and in the striving discover an infinity of new perspectives.

You might think about this: Jesus doesn't force the men he met on the road to go further. He doesn't tell these disciples: "Follow me." I don't know what he does tell them, but he achieves a paradox. *They are* the ones who say: "Follow us." But true faith is that area of freedom in which, step by step, God and man enter into an infinite communion. This area of freedom is created by the very distance that God defines when he approaches. God keeps his distance not because he is remote, but to prevent his nearness from being a constraint. God is omnipresent but he is not always "on our backs." He arouses in the disciples a desire for his Presence. Faith *is* desire: "Stay with us." Jesus readily complies. He enters. He enters, and makes us understand the Gospel by simply *staying*. He is there in order to be there. Jesus has stated: "Knock and it shall be opened to you." But it is ultimately *he* who knocks at *our* door. All that God seeks is to enter into our lives. Believing means: "Come in!" But how can God knock on a person's door if the person remains locked up within himself? How can God enter a person's house if one has no opening within himself? Saint Luke (Acts 14:27) speaks of the "door of faith." And indeed, faith presumes a certain visibility on the part of both God and man. If man needs signs of God's presence in order to meet God, then God likewise needs signs of *our* presence in order to meet us.

The instant one welcomes God within oneself, the real meaning of things begins to come clear: "Jesus broke the bread . . . and their eyes were opened." Their eyes were opened because their hearts were open, ready to receive what God had been preparing for them through all eternity: his own table in *their* houses. (They were at the inn, but they felt at home.) This sharing of bread has a resonance in the disciples, because it appeals to personal experience. The signs of faith are perceptible only to those who are ready to interpret them. The signs of faith are meaningless to nonbelievers. The Eucharist is the sign of Jesus Christ's presence for the person who is willing to recognize the sacrament of the Covenant in the consecrated bread. The bread is simply bread. It is mere appearance. What makes it a *sign* is that it is "consecrated," i.e. invested with the meaning that God gives it.

Believing is discerning the presence of God, who *always reveals himseslf through signs and beyond appearances*. This was what Christ tried to make us understand in his miracles. Remember Cana: "They have no more wine." Jesus pretends not to notice anything. He pretends to see nothing in order to make others see that there is something else. His mother intervenes. To her—to one who believes, who is faithful—he replies "invisibly," in a way that faith alone can understand: "My hour is not yet come." For others, he makes a visible gesture. Apparently, Jesus is the powerful man who has come to do great things. Saint John can say: "His glory was manifested." Which glory? The glory of the Easter mystery? But who discerned it? Mary? Perhaps—but what about the others at the feast? What did they see? A marvel—something wonderful? And yet it is just possible that they noticed nothing at all; for the visible sign of the miracle—if there was such a sign— was given in the kitchen. It would, in fact, be that wonderful but simple miracle that happened quietly in the kitchen at Cana, the one that prefigures some momentous things—baptism, the Eucharist, the Church, for instance. Who saw that this country wedding was the sign of the eternal union of God and humanity? Thus, the sign is deeper than outer appearance, and reality is vaster than the sign. Believing is measuring the distance between appearances, the sign, and reality. Beyond the *outer appearance* of this startling "emergency repair," and through the *sign* of water changed into wine, the hidden *reality* is revealed to us: *it is the mystery of the Covenant*. Discerning the signs given us by God, understanding what they mean, trying to see through God's own eyes what he reveals to us, and adjusting our eyes to his vision—these things help us to learn the faith in the most profound way.

• Dissecting Signs
The Reading of Signs

God reveals himself through the signs he has instituted: Word, Sacraments, Church, Charity, and so forth.

These are "official" signs, readily spotted. It is not always easy to know what God means to tell us in his Word and what he invites us to live in the church. Still, one can at least refer objectively to Revelation. In everyday life, however, we are prey to our own subjectivity. Who can assure us that a person we meet or an event we witness is truly a sign, and that it is a sign of God? Who can tell us that our love relationship with God is reciprocal, that we love God as God loves us? How, amid so many outward contradictions, are we to interpret the signs of God? Christians are always encouraged to spot the hand of God in the warp and woof of everyday life. But that is easier said than done. You really must dissect the signs, that is, peel away the superficial bark of appearances in order to draw out the sap of the significance of signs at their deepest level of meaning.

Do you want to know if what you experience is a sign of God? Begin by internalizing in yourself, for yourself, what you believe you have found in these signs. Don't ask yourself what Christ would have done in your place. He is *not* in your place. Each person must find his or her own place. Remember that the Spirit is in our hearts. Ask, rather, if your conduct in a given circumstance corresponds to what Christ tells us about the Holy Spirit: He is Truth, Freedom, Unity. In the discernment of signs, it is always the Spirit that helps us understand. "An unspiritual (thick) man," says Saint Paul to his obtuse Corinthians, "is one who does not accept anything of the Spirit of God. . . . A spiritual man, on the other hand, is able to judge the *value of everything*, and his *own value is not to be judged by other men*" (I Corinthians 2:14–15).

Do you understand the extraordinary, liberating force contained in this statement: Yes, indeed. If we are audacious enough to believe that life is an absolutely unique adventure in the Spirit, then we have enough certainty *not* to model our lives on what other people think. *Other people* really cannot understand the essence of *our* spiritual lives because *their* spiritual lives are different. Try discerning your own spiritual path, the route you are already following. Then, some day, you will have the experience of the road to Emmaus, walking with him on your own special path to understanding and enlightenment.

One of the dreariest aspects of life is that we meet so few free people: People who are free of the judgment of God, free of the judgment of others, free of their own judgment. "I hate you," says Camus in *Caligula*, "because you are not free." The resurrection is the road of freedom. If you really are convinced that you are acting in the freedom, the truth, and the unity of the Spirit, then you are probably in step with God and breathing with him on the road of life.

Knowledge and Recognition

After stopping to think about the discernment of signs, we should continue on our road, find the disciples again, and try to understand the meaning of their experience—and ours. The two companions don't suspect for an instant that the stranger is Jesus. They recognize him only at the breaking of the bread. Their hearts tremble: "No doubt about it: it is he."

But what do they really know of Christ? Have they already met him? We cannot be sure. We have every reason to believe that they were linked to Christ's own band of apostles. And since they say, "Some women from our group have astounded us," it seems likely that these two men are part of the group of followers around Jesus. They must have loved Jesus, their leader, if they are so distressed by his disappearance. But how do they love him? Perhaps as a guru whom one admired from afar, but whose message and teaching are immediate because his words are so deeply penetrating? Perhaps they feel about him as they would about a friend who is somewhat reclusive and not often available? All of these possibilities make sense. But it is still true that when a certain communion is established, then a certain vital experience is born. And isn't this vital experience the thing that permits the disciples on their way to Emmaus to recognize Christ through the sign of the Eucharist? We have no proof that the two men were present at the Last Supper on Holy Thursday. And yet nothing says they were *not* present. In any event, if they were not at the Last Supper they most likely had heard about it. Thus, the breaking of bread was undoubtedly an eloquent act for them. Even if they didn't help to celebrate the Last Supper, the breaking of bread would still evoke a whole, if unexplored, world. Faith is a world that we carry within us; a world that allows us to see and know Jesus.

When one is ready to *see* and *know*, really see and know, the sense of recognition can strike like lightning. At such an amazing moment men and women who have managed without God, discover in a flash that God was there, there in everything they have done or thought about doing. And the person who is converted (turned) in this way will always remember the exact moment of knowing, of recognition. *Faith is thus recognition before it becomes knowledge.* Faith is an encounter which always has something unexpected about it, however much one may have longed for its coming. Often two people will see that they were "made for each other" before they get to know each other well. This recognition of love, to be sure, does not exempt them from getting to know each other. But knowledge and recognition are concomitants. You can not peg the initial recognition of faith to knowledge. The child who receives a Christian upbringing from the cradle will experience God by first getting to know him, learning to understand who he is. A person coming to a recognition of God as an adult will often find him on the basis of the knowledge he gained in his childhood. And it is sad to note that most of the children who have not come to know God are incapable as well of recognizing him as adults. To state that *faith is recognition* is not to say that one cannot learn about God, cannot be educated in his ways; it merely stresses that if there is no constant turning of the heart in Christian life, no permanent conversion, one eventually becomes deadened to the faith; even if one knows God theoretically, one becomes incapable of recognizing the living Christ.

Food for the Road

If you take the road to Emmaus, you are taking your life and placing it in the hands of God. And these are the hands of the broken and shared bread, the hands that write a story. Believing means writing the story of your existence in God with every breath you draw, with every beat of your pulse. Because there is a shared story between man and God, an irresistible force linking man to the eternals of death and life, each one of us can be sure that his or her shared story forms an indestructible bond with God. This is a story that cannot be unwritten. Faith is something definitive and for all time. One cannot really lose faith. One may lose one's way or one's head. One may lose heart or lose one's bearing in the dark night of the soul, having failed to see the wonderful clarity inherent in the night.

Faith is a chiaroscuro, a mixture of dark and light. Rembrandt never understood this as clearly as he did on the day he painted the disciples of Emmaus. If we get to know the chiaroscuro of the faith, we will tame our darkness and learn to discern reality in the midst of shadows and dark imagining.

At the Easter Vigil, when we hear the cry of *"Beata nox!"* (Blessed night!), the whole church rejoices at discovering in the light of the Resurrected, the secret and invincible things that each person carries, locked within as provisions for the journey.

And what unique things these provisions are! If I fail to understand the precious gifts that can come to me through a relationship with the One God, the Unique God, it probably means I am not taking the right road. So long as I do not find my own special way of loving the Unique God, so long as I have done nothing that is truly real for the Unique God, I cannot know what the disciples mean when they speak of their burning hearts.

> God I Love you
> in my way.
> I love your loving me
> in your unique
> way.
>
> Unique God
> I love you uniquely
> As I love uniquely
> Him for being himself
> Her for being herself
> You
> I love you
> as one can love no one but You
>
> It is unique to love You uniquely.

2

Jesus: Someone to Find
Faith Is Seeking

As he walked along the road, he saw a man who had been blind from birth. His disciples asked him, "Rabbi, who sinned, this man or his parents, for him to have been born blind?" "Neither he nor his parents sinned," Jesus answered, "he was born blind so that the works of God might be shown in him.

> As long as the day lasts I must carry out the work of the one who sent me; the night will soon be here when no one can work. As long as I am in the world I am the light of the world.

Having said this, Jesus spat on the ground, made a paste of the dirt of the road and the spittle, and annointed the eyes of the blind man with the paste. He said to the blind man, "Go and wash in the Pool of Siloam" (Siloam is a name that means *sent*). So the blind man went to the pool and washed himself, and came away with his sight restored.

His neighbors and people who earlier had seen him begging said: "Isn't this the man who used to sit and beg?" Some said, "Yes, it is the same one." Others said, "No, he only looks like him." The man himself said, "I am the man."

So they said to him, "Then how do your eyes come to be open?" "The man called Jesus," he answered, "made a paste, daubed my eyes with it and said to me, 'Go and wash at Siloam'; and when I washed I could see." They asked "Where is he?" "I don't know," answered the man who had been blind.

They brought the man who had been blind to the Pharisees. It had been a sabbath day when Jesus made the paste and opened the man's eyes, so when the Pharisees asked him how he had come to see, he said, "He put a paste on my eyes, and I washed, and I can see." Then some of the Pharisees said, "This man cannot be from God; he does not keep the sabbath." Others said, "How could a sinner produce signs like this?" And there was disagreement among them. So they spoke to the blind man again, "What have you to say about him yourself, now that he has opened your eyes?" "He is a prophet," replied the man.

However, the Jews still would not believe that the man had been blind and had gained his sight, without first sending for his parents and asking them, "Is this man really your son who you say was born blind? If so, how is it that he is now able to see?" His parents answered, "We know he is our son and we know that he was born blind, but we don't know how it is that he can see now, or who opened his eyes. He is old enough: let him speak for himself." His parents said this out of fear of the Jews, who had already agreed to expel from the synagogue anyone who acknowledged Jesus as the Christ. This was why his parents said, "He is old enough; ask him."

So the Jews again sent for the man and said to him, "Give glory to God! For our part, we know that this man whom you say healed you is a sinner." The man answered, "I don't know if he is a sinner; I only know that I was blind and now I can see." They said to him, "What did he do to you? How did he open your eyes?" The man replied, "I have told you once and you wouldn't listen. Why do you want to hear it all again? Do you want to become his disciples too?" This made the Pharisees truly angry: "You can be his disciple," they said, "we are disciples of Moses: we know that God spoke to Moses, but as for this man, we don't know where he comes from." The man who had been blind replied, "Now here is an astonishing thing! He has opened my eyes, and you don't know where he comes from! We know that God doesn't listen to sinners, but God does listen to men who are devout and do his will. Ever since the world began it has been unheard of for anyone to open the eyes of a man who was born blind; if this man were not from God, he couldn't do a thing." "Are you trying to teach us," the Pharisees replied, "and you are a sinner through and through, since you were born!" And they drove him away.

Jesus heard they had driven away the man he had healed, and when he found him Jesus said to him. "Do you believe in the Son of Man?" "Sir," the man replied, "tell me who he is so that I may believe in him." Jesus said, "You are looking at him; he is speaking to you." The man said, "Lord, I believe," and worshiped him.

Jesus said:

> It is for judgment that I have come into this world, so that those without sight may see and those with sight turn blind.

Hearing this, some Pharisees who were present said to him, "We are not blind, surely?" Jesus replied,

> Blind? If you were, you would not be guilty, but since you say, "We see," your guilt remains.

(John 9)

The Grievance

All roads to Emmaus lead only to Jesus. Each and everyone of us has his road to Emmaus. On Christ's road, we all meet one another. We learn to recognize one another. You are, I am, we are—the deaf, the dumb, the stammering, the paralyzed, the possessed, the blind.

The tale about the cure of the man born blind is the story of a judgment. The opening of a trial. The trial of Jesus. Jesus will not go very much further now. Everything he does, every move he makes is watched. But he will see it through. Everything will not be done by Good Friday.

Will the accused rise! Jesus! Jesus, the eternally accused, you are not pardoned, you have never been pardoned for daring to disturb our night! But you are the Light of the World, you say. Who are you to make such a claim? People ask this question of you—but they really do not wish to know the answer.

Ultimately, the true crime charged in this trial is that God reveals himself as Light. The Judge of Light. The inquiry proceeds, but there is a dramatic turn of events. The defendant becomes the judge. The judge judges all of us: "It is for judgment that I have come into this world, so that those without sight may see and those with sight turn blind." Jesus is dreadful.

· The Judgment
The Master of Justice

No one is blinder than the man who does not wish to see. But God blinds no one. He simply shows us that we have put out our own eyes. God rejects no one. He shows us that it is people who have separated themselves from God. When God judges, he does not condemn. He exposes us to the light. This unmasking is the work of the Spirit: "When he comes (the Advocate, the Spirit of Truth) he will show the world how wrong it was, about sin and about who was in the right, and about judgment"(John 16:8). The Master of Justice is the Spirit, for the justice of the world is not *of* this world. No man can judge. God alone is the judge, because God the Spirit is also God the Father. Christ calls us to order: "Do not judge, for when you judge, you become the jailors of your brothers." Yes, inevitably, we enclose the other in our judgment. We hobble him with our own limitations. We freeze him in place so that we can control him. We "make up our minds" about him and in so doing imprison him within our own limitations. This is why Christ himself does not judge. Only his Word serves to judge us. And the Word comes from the Father. "The word itself that I have spoken will be his judge on the last day"(John 12:48). At the very heart of the Word, there is virtually a distance between the person of the Son of God and his mission as an envoy of the Father. "If anyone hears my words and does not keep them faithfully, *it is not I* who shall condemn him, since I have come not to condemn the world, but to save the world: he who rejects me and refuses my words has *his* judge already"(John 12:47–49).

People today do not want to be judged. Not even by God—least of all by God. We understand that man rebels against a Judge-God when he catches himself in *flagrante delicto* judging God in the same way that we judge our fellowman. It's no use repeating by rote that God judges with love—the human allergy remains. And how tenacious this rejection of a Judge-God is. Too many of the Roman Catholic Jansenists or Protestant Puritans among us have been marked by the threat of the Last Judgment, the obsession with condemnation, the fear of divine wrath.

Still, today one no longer can say that Christians are traumatized by the fear of this Terrible God. How many, for instance, applauded a popular entertainer when he sang: "We'll all go to heaven." The public needs reassurance from whatever source. After all, you're a lot more appealing if you sing promises than if you hurl anathemas! One can only rejoice at this universal kindliness: Yes, let's banish the Pharisaism of the virtuous prudes who monopolize the right to enter paradise. We all agree that morality alone has never brought anyone through the pearly gates. We will all be judged, of course, but we'll all get together again up there at mankind's best party ever!

You're not being a wet blanket if you wonder about the validity of this big collective ticket to Paradise. We'll all go to heaven! If this means that our present life has no meaning, no value, no importance, then I'd rather not go. The writer of "We'll all go to heaven" and all the people who hum it won't go that far, of course. But if you want to grasp what God's judgment means, then perhaps you should first recall the price of life: What I do with my life, right or wrong, matters to God!

Believing in God the Judge means beginning to believe in the value of one's own actions. Believing in God the Judge means believing that God recognizes each human being in a unique way. Believing in God the Judge means opening ourselves to a Mercy that will amaze us with its understanding, with its perception of who we are. But no one is totally exempt from judgment.

A Passerby Different from All Others

The story of the man who was blind from birth begins with a harmless word: "Passing by . . . . " Passing by, says the Gospel, Jesus sees a man who was born blind. This phrase might just be inserted to smoothe out the style. The Gospels frequently jump from one subject to another. A chapter is finished, how do you start the next one? You need a transition. These opening words might also express a certain randomness: Well, one day, Jesus happened to be passing by when he ran into a blind man. However, if you're at all familiar with Saint John, the most mystical and most precise of the Evangelists, the most symbolic and also the most historical, then everything tells you that this phrase is not fortuitous: it locates everything concretely, and everything is charged with a meaning that goes beyond the banality of the words.

"Passing by": this locates things in time and space; where they happen concretely, on the road. It also situates things on a different level of reality, for the road is not just any road; the road *is* Jesus. Jesus is he who by his death and Resurrection established the passage from darkness to light. This is the road that Jesus will have the blind man take. Thus, while passing by, Jesus saw a man. Nothing escapes Jesus. In the spontaneity of the instant, his attentive mind seizes on something that could be sheer coincidence and that becomes the setting of an encounter with God. While, to all appearances, nothing has led Jesus to this meeting, the fate of the blind man is decided in the twinkling of an eye.

Believing means learning to read the events of your life as the expression of God's passage. You let God pass. You make your life this passage. You pass your life seeking the road. And then one day, you come face to face with a Passerby who is not like anyone else. Believing means opening your eyes on that day and murmuring, "Hello, my Lord and my God."

The Blind Man, a Witness for the Defense

In the many Gospel tales about cures, it is usually the sick person himself or the people with him who call for Jesus. Remember the leper: "Lord, if you want to, you can cure me"; the centurion's servant: "Just say one word"; Jairus: "My daughter is dead, come"; the blind man of Jericho: "Lord, make me see!"

However, the man born blind is a different case. Jesus does not wait for the blind man to beseech him. He makes the first move himself. "I didn't ask your advice. Go wash yourself." Why does Jesus appear to be so forceful and determined. Because he is about to be arraigned before a mortal tribunal. He has to hurry. He knows that the Pharisees want to corner him. They demand proof. So he'll have to give them some; not to clear himseslf in their eyes, but, as Saint John reports (9:3): "So that the works of God might be shown in him."

This trial is an apocalypse. God reveals himself in Jesus Christ as Light. And to do so, Jesus has recourse to a blind man, an invalid, a pauper, as a witness for the defense. But he doesn't exploit the blind man. He is personally interested in him. Saint John even notes as much. The first thing that Jesus notices is not the blind man who will serve his argument, but the *man* himself. This is well translated in the Gospel by the preeminence accorded to the man. The Gospel does not say "Jesus saw a blind man." It says: "Jesus saw a man *who* was blind." This relative pronoun tells us that the basic antecedent for God is always man.

The Eloquence of the Poor

The blind man has the reactions of a beggar. He is the person who waits indefinitely. He must wonder what is happening to him. He allows everything to happen to him without quite understanding. He accepts the sign that for us Westerners seems devoid of any meaning. Jesus spits. Not very sanitary. He makes mud with his saliva. Not very appetizing. But in the Semitic world of those days it was a powerful symbol; saliva is the breath of life. Mud recalls the primal clay, the mud of life. This symbolism is ultimately beautiful; but here and now, the sign is poor, crude, even ludicrous. Jesus could have uttered a solemn word in an august gesture, an "Open Sesame" whose secret would be known to him alone. But God's true power is shown by this habit of his—since his birth on straw and his death on wood—to offer *poor* signs. The poverty of these signs is eloquent. God does not impose himself by means of grand exploits. He proposes humble gestures that demand transparency and recognition. The blind man obeys without hesitation: no faith is possible without this deliberate and docile confidence. Taking the path of faith means agreeing to see God reveal himself through signs whose outer appearances are often disconcerting. There is nothing depersonalizing about this docility. Our blind man turns out to be quite a person. What good sense! What a fine sense of humor!

He's called to the witness stand, before a panel of solid citizens. The Pharisees, with all the dignity of their tradition of high principles, ask him for his testimony. Like Jesus, the blind man has the eloquence of poor people with full hearts. He tells his story with the finest popular verve. Gives it to them straight. Pulls no punches: " Hell, I didn't usta see, now I ken see—what's yer problem?" He's put his finger on the sore spot, the sore spot of the Pharisees. He understands very well that they don't much care for his cure. The Pharisees question the blind man—not to learn the truth, but to fulfill their own worst suspicions. The blind man sees clearly. He tells the Pharisees their truth: "It's no use talking to you. You don't listen." And with an irony verging on sarcasm, he asks them whether they might not like to become disciples of Jesus Christ themselves!

The blind man teaches us how to find Christ. Let God do what he has to do, even if it means making mud out of our rather sorry lives. Getting up early, walking in the dark until we reach the dawn of a new day. At some point in life, there comes a moment when the light is seen, perceived, received for itself: God. If we want to find this light, the light which give eyes to the blind man, shouldn't we simply, quite simply, so very simply, bow to the facts? The call of faith then becomes audible: "Do you believe in the Son of Man?" asks Jesus. The question inevitably comes in a direct encounter. As pinpointed by Saint John, Jesus, upon meeting the blind man, ask, "Do you believe in the Son of Man?"

And the blind man's reply: "Sir, tell me who he is so that I may believe in him."

The dialogue becomes personal. Jesus is not content to anwer: "The Son of Man is God, and I am his Envoy." He says: "You are looking at him; he is speaking to you." Seeing is believing; seeing not only with the eyes, but with the entire being, with the heart, the intelligence, the whole life force. Sooner or later, in some way or other, experiencing the invincible evidence of the living reality of Christ—this is part of the experience of faith. It means suddenly seeing with a new intensity, like someone familiar with the seashore who sees the same ocean day after day—and then one day, watching the tide come in, sees a wonderful new color in the sky—an unimagined and almost indescribable blue.

Day and night: This is a theme dear to Jesus. At the start of this Gospel, he declares rather oddly: "As long as this day lasts I must carry out the work of the one who sent me; the night will soon be here when no one can work." Some people indeed open their eyes the instant they close them, when the sun of life is setting. But no matter, for, as Christ says, "so long as I am in the world, I am the Light of the World." These words, even though they are spoken before his Resurrection, are always to have meaning. They attempt to tell us in a paradoxical manner: We have all the time in the world, and at the same time, we have no time to lose. The search for faith has no deadline, but we all run the risk of losing the thread of our search if it goes on too long, prey to the traps and snares of over-intellectualizing and evasion as we humans always are. We run the risk of protracting our search into the night the Gospel speaks of, the time ". . . when no one can work." One seeks in order to find, not for the satisfaction of being a seeker. But, Jesus will inevitably appear before the mortal tribunal, no matter where we are in our personal journey.

He turns the trial upside down. All you witnesses, the people: Defendants, rise! I. You. We. Everyone. Who dares to open his eyes and look upon the face of God? Who is willing to take the full force of that unimaginable light directly in his or her face, letting it break over you as a wave would if you stood on the deck of a boat during a storm? Really, whoever we are, we are all the blind man—the parents, the neighbors, the disciples, and the Pharisees. And Judas is already lurking in the shadows and drawing nearer. All of us are part of the shaky world; the world within us all where a million human dramas are played out. Let's go to the tribunal.

• The Jurors
The Parents:
People Who Don't Want to Get Involved

Their reflex is that of Pilate: Our son was blind? Ask him. "It's for you to see. He's old enough to talk, to speak for himself. And you're old enough to talk to him." Pilate didn't want to get involved. And they don't want to either. No complications. They are afraid of being kicked out of the synagogue. They are frightened. You really can't be frightened *and* have faith at the same time. Faith is confidence. You don't look for God in fear, you will only find him in confidence.

But you have to admit that these parents extricate themselves from the situation nicely. They have the advantage of being able to say, "We're leaving our boy alone, he can answer for himself!" They disengage themselves. When you are just not there, you can't do anything wrong—you simply do nothing at all. That's the tragedy of today's Christians. Christians who are nice, inoffensive, wouldn't harm a fly, Christians who never rock the boat—that's what many of us are becoming or have become.

The Neighbors: People with Their Habits

These people are busybodies with a taste for gossip. They are anxious to find out whether or not the agitated fanatic they see before them is really the beggar who has always sat in this same place—or is he just a lookalike. But do you think they ask about Jesus? About the meaning of the cure? No, these people, most people, are far more curious about *how* things have happened than they are about what they mean. Unfortunately, this is quite normal and harmless. There's no harm in reading some terrible tabloid newspaper, but there *is* harm in seeing life only through that dreadful sheet. To employ the term in the Gospel, these people who are *accustomed* to seeing the blind man are so utterly *accustomed* that they remain on a very superficial level of understanding and awareness, the level of credulity, which arouses the incredulity of others. Superficiality is one of the chief obstacles to faith. It's like hearing a depressing story about an infant being suffocated accidentally by the luxurious eiderdown quilt spread over him without his ever waking. A lot of us have been bundled up in equally treacherous eiderdowns for years now! Just look at the series of conflicts that were aroused by the Roman Catholic Church's abandonment of Latin in the mass, by the trend toward administering communion in the hand, by the growing practice of lay people (suitably licensed) distributing communion, by the growing number of priests who have ceased to wear cassocks, and by the legions of nuns appearing out of habit and sometimes in trousers. And we won't even discuss the internal quarrels in parishes, the doctrinal disputes of factions within the church—and scores of other things. Tell me: Where is Christ in all this? Confined to the little place in which we have locked him up. Our superficiality imprisons God in the exteriors and surfaces of the church. We are frightened by the simplicity of the Gospel, and we dare not *invent* the love that Christ expects from us. We confine faith to the habits of faith, and when we lose the habits of faith, we are astonished at not finding God still in his customary, usual place. *God is never customary.* One does not look for God by brooding over the ways we have tried to seek him in the past. One finds him in new things, in adventures and missions that remain to be done.

The Disciples: People with Principles

They mean well, those people who think the other fellow is always the sinner. Who has sinned? They do not bother asking why this man is blind. They already know that. If he's blind, he must have sinned. It would probably not cross their minds to look at the facts. The issue is *not* one of sin. They don't even consider that possibility. They react in an almost programmed, predictable way. In those days, people regarded disease and infirmity as divine punishment. We cannot reproach them for being of their time and judging by the criteria of their society; but we can regret that their nearness to Christ did not help them see further. We can't reproach today's Christians for having had yesterday's catechism, and reacting in terms of a specific upbringing; but we can regret that the breath of the Spirit, as expressed in the present renewal of the church, has not yet swept the formalism of a moralizing faith from their consciences. Admittedly, this formalism seems to be receding, but one might speculate rather cynically about whether or not that phenomenon has more to do with the diminishing number of Christians in the world, all told. But what about those who remain? Do they try to understand how one can live in good faith with the Gospel in an ambiguous, contradictory situation, or do they simply judge like the disciples, who referred to "principles?" There's nothing wrong with principles. They merely express the values of the Gospel. If Christians have principles, it means that they draw their rules for life from the Gospel; that's fine, too. But if they are "people of principles," this means that they, like the Pharisees, are attached to the letter of the law, forgetting the Spirit. A principle adhered to for its own sake can become just another stumbing block in the search for God.

The Pharisees: Prim and Proper People

They are extremists of a sort. Enough has probably been said about them. They are usually thought of as self-righteous caricatures or as monsters of harshness. But one shouldn't exaggerate. It's true that Christ has little patience with them. He calls them hypocrites, dead men, a race of vipers. He tells them they will surely come to no good. But in point of fact, the Pharisees are the professional legalists; extremists on the subject of the integrity of the law. And there is such a thing as good "integrists." Yet it's hard for them not to have a legalistic reflex . As custodians of a body of applied laws, they are always inclined to find the truth ensconced securely in the past. When they cite the past, it's to demonstrate that it has nothing to do with the present. They reject firmly the newness of the Now of Jesus Christ. Their formalism crystallizes around the observance of the sabbath and they have hit upon a pretext for their accusation. This strikes us as disproportionate and unfair. And yet, for a long time, wasn't the value of Christian life judged according to faithful patterns of religious practice? A good practitioner was synonymous with a good Christian. A good practitioner, doing charitable works, was translated as a "great Christian." Irreproachable on the level of practice, which they view as the sole standard of faithfulness, the Pharisees dare to judge the secrets of other peoples' hearts and souls.

What person can venture to say about another that he or she is a sinner? Christ never went that far at any point in the

Gospels. When he tells the adulteress "Go and sin no more," it is not to confuse her, but to assure her that conversion is possible and hope permissible. This does not mean that Christ has no use for the virtuous or takes their goodnesses lightly. But he wants us to understand that *beyond* fine principles, the person whose heart is not hardened will always have the hope of conversion. Hardening of the heart is the main obstacle to conversion, not sin. You *can't* turn a hardened heart. Many Christians, who have good hearts in official works of charity, fail to realize that their hearts may be hard in their everyday lives. And this is a real hindrance, one of the hindrances that keeps any number of contemporary people from finding Christ. For hardening of the heart can engender the self-complacency that Saint John repeatedly notes, the mad pretention of people who say: "We know. We know that you've spoken to Moses! We know that you do not give ear to the sinners. . . ." In other words: "We have the light, we have the monopoly on truth." And this is what makes Christ so sad: "If you were blind, you would be without sin, but you say: 'We see.' and your sin remains."

The Verdict

Our trial began in light. At the very start, Christ proclaimed: "I am the Light of the World." The judgment is passed at night. The last words are dark: "Your sin remains."

Jesus has lost the trial. Everything is played out. Everything is judged. The Pharisees *have* won, but they *are doomed*. The trial that they win condemns them. They are dead. Jesus does not triumph at their invisible defeat. He does not want to see even his accusers locked forever in death. He, too, will know death and pass through it. Jesus will die so that his death will end the despair of all of those who have died and will die. Jesus *converts* death. He says a

definitive *no* to damnation. Jesus has come to seek what was
lost, so that in each of us a Judas hopes.

Jesus	I am Judas	You are Jesus
Jesus	I am a coward	Judas
	Don't release me	
	Dwell on me	
	I love you	
	Jesus judge me	
	with a kiss	

3

Jesus: Someone Provocative
Faith Is a Scandal

He was setting out on a journey when a man ran up, knelt before him and asked him this question: "Good master, what must I do to have eternal life?" Jesus said to him, "Why do you call me good? No one is good but God alone. You know the commandments: *You must not kill; You must not commit adutery; You must not steal; You must not bear false witness; You must not cheat; You must honor your father and mother.*" And he said to him, "Master, I have observed all these things from my earliest days." Jesus looked steadily at him and loved him, and he said, "There is one thing you have not done. Go and sell everything you own and give the money to the poor, and you will have treasures in heaven; then come, follow me." But the man's face fell at these words and he went away sad, for he was a man of great wealth. (Mark 10:17–22)

The Way of the Cross

Taking the road to Emmaus is taking the road of the cross. You can only find the road to the resurrection by experiencing the cross. "You want to live, you want to believe? Take the cross." On the road of faith the cross is the loose rock which causes you to fall. The really outrageous, scandalous thing is that faith is linked inseparably to the cross! You can't hold onto life and love the cross. The really strange thing is that life itself is crucified.

In the Gospels the cross is revealed in demands that seem inhuman, through paradoxes that make us uncomfortable and puzzle us. Here are some very strong words from the Gospels: "If any man comes to me without hating his father, mother, wife, children, brothers, sisters, yes, and his own life, too, he cannot be my disciple" (Luke 14:26). This is an intensely Semitic way of putting things, an exaggerated manner of speaking to bring home the point that God is absolute. Clearly, God has not come to preach hatred. But, we must understand that one can prefer *nothing else* to God. And if you think about it, you know that sometimes thinking of God before and above everything else can quite literally mean the cross—the crucifixion of our very lives.

"It is not peace that I come to bring, but a sword" (Matthew 10:34). This is a paradox. God has not come to declare war. Jesus means: "You will be hated on account of my name" (Matthew 10:22). When a person chooses Jesus, he or she will be rejected by some of their closest relatives. Because of Jesus, there may be discord in families. "I have come to set a man against his father, a daughter against her mother, a daughter-in-law against her mother-in-law. A man's enemies will be those of his own household" (Matthew 10:34–36). But Christ has come not to sow discord, but to tell us: "You must make a choice. He who is not with me is against me." Everyone knows that choosing God within one's home is, at certain moments, an experience, in a very real way, of the cross.

"If your eye should cause you to sin, tear it out: it is better for you to enter into the Kingdom with one eye than to have two eyes and be stopped at the gate" (Matthew 18:9). A flash of wit, not to be taken literally! Christ means: "There is nothing more important than the Kingdom!" It's worth sacrificing everything to it. But this still doesn't mean that you should tear out your eyes. Otherwise, in this kingdom of the one-eyed and blind, everyone will be king. Everyone knows that sacrificing even your own body, your own life is, at certain moments, the cross.

"Anyone who wants to save his life will lose it; but anyone who loses his life for my sake will find it" (Matthew 16:25). This is a provocation. God tells us what the Gospel commits us to: the cross. One can twist these flashes of wit, turn the paradoxes, infer nuances—but there's no waffling on this mapped-out road: "If anyone wants to be a follower of mine let him . . . take up his cross and follow me" (Matthew 16:24). It's clear.

Such language is harsh. Who can permit it? Failure to use such language is betrayal. "Woe unto me," said Saint Paul, "if I do not preach Christ and Christ crucified."

• The Cross. God's Dimension on Earth
The Tree of Life

The cross is the special symbol of Christianity. The Christian is the person who makes the sign of the cross. The sign of the cross is not a formal sign. It is a brutal reality. Faith is suspended on the cross. Faith is there because the cross is there. The cross is there because God rose up again. The cross would be a senseless sign if it were the cross of a dead God. The cross is not a bier on which we display a corpse. The Resurrection is the fruit of the tree of life; the tree of life is the cross—the tree of the knowledge of God. It is the cross that showed us what God was like and how far he would go with us: all the way to the Resurrection is the answer. One cannot separate the cross and the Resurrection.

If we try to forget about the cross, hide it away on the
pretext that the "finale"—the Resurrection—is what counts
—this means treating the cross as though it were purely a
means to an end. The cross is *not* a means to an end. It is *not*
a kind of tool that God found marvelously useful for the redemption of sin. The cross is not a sort of trick of God's. It
is, in fact, God's dimension on earth. It is not an intermedi-
ary between God, who redeems, and man, who is redeemed.
It is the human-divine space, the unique space of the Resurrection. The cross is not an accident in Christ's life—the final, fatal accident; it is the core, the central point of God's
life in Jesus Christ made man. It is an expression of love. It is
part of the language of divine love through which God
wanted to express the inexpressible. But how can one penetrate the absolute freedom of God, who wanted to show the
gratuitousness of his love through the apparent madness of
a crucified love?

It is only this willingness to love that allows us not to justify the cross (for God himself does not justify it) but to welcome the mystery of it. If the cross is not love, then faith
risks being reduced to some sort of sado-masochistic relationship. Our God is not a sado-masochistic God who enjoys suffering in order to redeem man, and who also de-
lights in seeing man forced to suffer in order to be redeemed.

Certainly, our era is more sensitive to the Resurrection
than to the cross. Let's be frank. Do people talk about the
Resurrection to go with the times or to invite Christians to
live their faith in its baptismal fullness; that is, to make each
life a passage from death to life? One does not speak properly about the Resurrection unless one lives properly in
terms of the cross. It's our job to rediscover the meaning of
the cross by looking point-blank at the most scandalous love
story of all time!

Madness!

The cross is a torture. There is no cross without a drawing and quartering. The cross is a torment. There is no cross without humiliation. The cross is abject. Jesus was struck by *the* cross the day it became *his* cross. For God, the cross was the stumbling block he himself had ordained. For us, the cross is the obstacle of obstacles. "Such madness in the world, that's what God chose to confuse the sages and wise men." Yes, madness. Why did God choose to be mad? The cross is God's provocation, not because it hurts, but because it goes *against nature*. It wounds us. It kills us. But we also know that the cross has Salvation inherent in it; it is only truly the cross if it becomes the Tree of the Resurrection. Then it becomes Glorious. "Our one reliance," sings the liturgy of Good Friday, because it *is* the only source from which Life can spring.

Easily said. The passage really is too easy to say. Christians use ready-made words and phrases. They've got an answer for everything. Because they feel they already have the revelation, they anticipate it with pat reactions. It appears all too simple: a magic trick. The cross and the Resurrection—"presto chango" and it's done. We may look as if we're juggling with words, but there's a point to be made. The Resurrection is tied to the cross, but that doesn't make the cross any lighter. The Risen Christ does not say: "There was nothing to the cross!" When he reappears we see that his body was pierced, nail holes are there in his feet and hands. The cross is madness. God doesn't brag about it or flaunt it. His response is silence. He doesn't explain it. He simply asks us to see the New World around us where his cruel tree has borne fruit. He asks us to experience it. He sets us on our path. He shows us how living the cross means denying oneself. The cross and renunciation are one and the same. Again: "If anyone wants to be a follower of mine, let him *renounce* himself and take up his *cross* and follow me."

· You're Never Quits with God
Wild about Everything and Cherishing Nothing

But how can one take the cross? God isn't very concrete. He doesn't say concretely what end you should pick it
up by. No instructions on how to carry it. God does not enclose the Mystery of the Cross (*the Redemption*) in rules to
observe or things to do. The cross is planted in the heart of
each life. It is "made flesh" in each of us. "Each man has his
cross to bear," we are told. That is why the evangelists did
not say that a man has to take *the* cross, but *his* cross. God
waits for us at that moment in our lives where, in order to
say yes to God, we must say no to ourselves. Deny ourselves.
Self-denial is not loss of self. It is a remaking of ourselves
so we may become new in Christ. It is the way of Christ
Resurrected. Self-denial is the way we move from death to
ourselves to life in Christ. It is a way of freeing ourselves
from ego; it opens the way to personal liberation. Like the
cross, self-denial is not a set path or mode for living with
Christ. And it is not necessary to deprive oneself uselessly.
But think of some images and they may help you understand self-denial: think of the grain that rots and dies in
order to bear fruit; think of the tropism of life, the natural
movement of living things towards the brightest sunlight.
And by tropism in this case, I mean the sort of wisdom, the
sort of calm acceptance that quite naturally moves towards
the most complete spiritual flowering. Renunciation does
not mean resignation, it means saying "yes" to the real
nature of things and saying it willingly and happily.
There is no asceticism without mysticism. The thing
missing among many Christians today is not imagination,
the imagination to invent new ascetic practices; there is a
lot of that around. What's missing is the ability to achieve
real depth of mystical experience and with that depth a real
understanding of the Easter faith. The odd thing is that our

ordinary, everyday life experiences can sometimes open spiritual doors that esoteric ascetic practices may fail to open. Sometimes these experiences may on the surface, be painful or even cruel—but they have been known to bring people face to face with the Holy Spirit. Sometimes fate steps in and confronts people with illness, or deformity, the loss of a spouse, sterility, forced celibacy. All these can be seen as a terrible blow to endure or disabilities to overcome. But they can also bring about a release, a new life.

I am also thinking of the situations that one accepts by free choice: the research physician who gives up a lucrative career; the artist who remains faithful to his art rather than becoming a star; the priest who has the opportunity to be a religious innovator but instead chooses to inconspicuously serve the church in the usual way; the monk who takes on celibacy willingly as a path to greater fruitfulness. A person who practices self-denial is not a cripple. This person may well be truly free.

Self-denial does not mean forfeiting one's life. When Christ spoke to the rich man who had everything, he said: "You lack something. The thing you lack is to know lack. Paradoxically, what you lack is Poverty. . . ."

Anything But That!

This following scene in the Gospel aptly illustrates what renunciation means. God leaves us without a leg to stand on: "Drop everything . . . you have a treasure in heaven!" God summons us. Down here, we are already destined for a higher life. For holiness. Holiness is not moral perfection. Holy does not mean irreproachable. Holiness, like a rose, can blossom on a dung heap. The saint is not the man who can boast of being "impeccable" in the current sense of the word. Holy, saintly, according to its Semitic root, means "separate." "I am God and not man; in your midst, I am the Holy" (Hosea 11:9). For man, being saintly does not mean separating himself from his humanhood and becoming some kind of angelic being. It means saying "no" to everything that prevents us from being as human as Jesus, the Christ, was human. Being saintly means being human *with* God.

The rich man, it seems, knows Christ well. His genuflexion is a true profession of faith. One might even think that when talking to Christ, he lays it on a bit thick, behaving in a classic "holier-than-you" way. The rich man calls Jesus, "Good master." To which Jesus replies: "Why do you call me good? Only God is good. Thus, you acknowledge that I can ask anything of you!" This Jew—assuming he recognized Jesus as the Messiah—could still not have recognized who he was in the full sense we have when we speak of Jesus as the Lord. But he does admit that Jesus can make God's absolute demands upon him. But, Jesus asks nothing unusual or special of the rich man. He asks only that he obey the most basic of commandments: "You know the commandments: don't kill, don't commit adultery, don't steal, and so on . . . . " This (let's not talk of natural law or natural morality) is the map of a possible world. Experience tells us that a world in which people kill is not viable. To share in the eternal life, God suggests that we first understand what life on earth is all about. The rich man replies: "The good life here on earth was the joy of my youth. But isn't there something else?" The rich man needs something else. He actually senses that *faith* is different from *faithfulness* to natural law and to morality.

Jesus respects the first halting steps to awareness that the rich man takes. But he challenges him to go further. Jesus gauges the intensity of the man's hunger for faith, and he is also aware of the immensity of what he, Jesus, will ask of him. As on the road to Emmaus, Jesus keeps his distance for a while. This distance is marked by the intensity of his gaze: "Jesus stared at him and loved him." This is one of the most poignant sentences in the Gospels. What happens in this gaze? And how does the man look at God, who looks at him? The eyes of God in the eyes of man. It is not written: "Jesus looked at him because he loved him." The Gospel notes a curious progression. Jesus stared *and* loved him. Taking the time to love, the time to scrutinize, Christ discovers that he loves him and loves him more than he thought. Not only does Jesus respect the path that this man has begun to follow, but Jesus himself agrees to move along, to go further. He has gone further in love, because he has gone further in the time of loving. There is no private path to faith. God walks with man. Thus, as when one has something difficult to say, Christ "gives it to him straight" at one fell swoop: "You really want to know? Well, here it is. . . . I wouldn't have told you if you hadn't asked. . . . There's one thing you lack: go and sell what you have, give it to the poor, and you'll have a treasure in heaven. Come and follow me!"

There's one thing you lack. It's not some optional thing, one of those things you can add on to something else. It's not one more degree of perfection to attain. It is the heart of things: the cross. The demand for poverty that Christ presents to the rich young man strikes at the most precious thing he has. And not only at what he has, but also at what he is. Christ means: "Don't be less than you can be!" The young man then says what we ourselves so often say: "Anything but that!" We strike God as he struck us in paradise: we too have our tree that must not be touched, and we say to God: "If you touch it, then we will no longer be masters of our destiny!" The truth is that God does not respect private property. At all the entrances to our patches of life, we put up signs. "Beware of dog," "No trespassing." But it is no use. Christ steps over across barriers and tells us: "Leave everything!" Such is the audacity of God. He summons us to holiness. Being holy means planting your tree outside the paradise *you* choose; it means transplanting it where God wants it, pruning it, realizing that it's only got stumps, like trees pruned back in the spring, before Easter. No more branches, just two arms. The naked cross!

The cross is a pruned tree. The cross always provokes us to the very core of our existence. For the rich young man, his cross is poverty. For someone else, it's something else. The authenticity of our search for God is tested out not in the way we settle the questions that faith asks of us theoretically, but in the way we allow God to interfere actively in our lives. The rich young man is likeable, honest. He doesn't justify his own inability to say yes by citing a similar disability in others. He doesn't excuse himself by blaming his own mediocrity on the institutions of the church or on intellectual grounds.

Christ then declares: "You will have treasures in heaven." This is not compensation, not bargaining; this is placing the cross in the dimension of the Resurrection. Christ tells him: "If you agree to live by passing across the death that this property signifies, you will discover what treasures I mean." At these words, the night invades this man. He becomes gloomy. He goes away in sadness, sadness at the impossible. But there was much that was good about him, the Gospel says.

Leave Everything!

"Leave everything." One feels like saying it's impossible to do that. It's inhuman. But God is not inhuman. He does *not* exact the impossible. By telling the rich man, "Leave everything," God is not browbeating him. He is meeting the man's hopes halfway. This man, so avid for God, expects Jesus to say: "God is Everything. If God can ask everything of you, it is because he gives you everything." When God asks everthing of man, God honors him. God reveals to man that man is everything to him. If God did not believe in man, he would not ask everything of him. If God did not hope for the new human being that Christ brought into being, he would continue to prescribe the ancient Law. But God has shattered all prescriptions and has invented a new kind of freedom, creative freedom.

"Leave everything." One might translate this evangelical summons with the famous words of Saint Augustine: "Love and do what you wish." In the category of love, you're never through with the person you love. God has shattered the old regime of the Pharisees; there's no going back. In the Law, you can imagine that you've "done your duty" if you live up to the Law. But who can really keep every commandment always,—who can pride themselves on *always* being consistent with the law. But the Law can be a trap, says Saint Paul, because it shows man that he is incapable of fully observing it.

"Leave everything." But Jesus did not come to crush man's hope by demanding of him something he cannot do. He came to challenge mankind to grow in his love. One does not grow all at once. A long nail is driven in with short blows. "Leave everything" is a categorical imperative, to be sure, but it stretches out in time. Following Christ takes a lifetime. The disciple walks step by step. The disciple is walking with Christ to reach the center of his own life in Christ. Once on this joyous path, there is no stopping and no turning back.

"Leave everything" is a call to reject the aimlessness of the mediocre, the smugness of the satisfied, the asphyxia of the intoxicated. Over and over again, we hear that we live in a polluted atmosphere. The material, mundane things of life hold us back, weigh us down, stick to us like glue. The Gospel constantly tells us to come *unglued* from ourselves, to break free.

The Gospel's call to break free, to come loose, is not idle words for pious people. It is a desperately important and

crucifying demand; the Way of the disciple is called the
Easter road. To detach oneself, according to the Gospel, is
one of the ways to incarnate the death and Resurrection of
Christ in one's own life. To detach oneself is to die in terms
of oneself, not in order to be buried alive in self-denial, but,
on the contrary, to live more fully in the freedom of the
Spirit. We are asked to rediscover self-denial as the living
movement of the Spirit in us, which makes us say no to anything that keeps us from being fully human. However,
watch your step! Being "detached" doesn't mean looking
gloomy and mournful. In that case you might be better off
more "attached" and a little joyful. One is more authenti-
cally *detached*, according to the Gospel, if one is more gen-
uinely attached and loving of life, its goods, its joys, its fan-
tasies. The attachment to the things of life can be a stimulus
to life. The person who is indifferent to everything is just
vegetating. The person to whom nothing has any meaning
ultimately lets himself die.

The Gift of the Cross

The way in which you deal with the cross deter-
mines, ultimately, the way in which you live. The cross
leads us to choose the true self in which the Risen Christ can
be truly realized. God keeps asking more and more today so
that tomorrow we may be more fulfilled in our faith than
we were yesterday. Our aspiration toward the infinite is inspired by a God who is infinite beyond our wildest imagin-
ings and most fervent aspirations. The success of our aspiration to spiritual attainment is in proportion to our ultimate
hunger for God's infinity. Believing means harmonizing.
God's absolute desire must harmonize or come together
with the strength of our human aspiration. Because of the
Kingdom, because of the Word, because of the infinite will
of God, Christ enables us to attain some portion of our heritage. The prayer of the "good rich man," according to the

Gospel, is the cry of the naive person who suddenly understands the wonders that God has worked in him—despite everything, despite his human weakness. For finally and at last, despite our struggles, we must give thanks for the cross, which is a great gift.

Lord
because of the Kingdom. . . .
like you,
I spoke:
I could not silence cowardice.

And then, also like you, I kept silent
because at certain times one must keep silent:
I did not open my mouth before stupidity;
I did not want to scandalize the weak man;
yet I did not seek to justify everything either.
I did not have the last word, because of you! . . .

Because of your Word. . .
I said yes and the truth set me free
I said no and I was sent back . . .
I dared and the stones cried out. . . .

Because of you
I renounced, not everything, but still. . . .
I left, not everything, but still. . . .
I lost, not everything, but still. . . .
I found the cross, and beyond. . . .
The road. The Truth. Life.

4

Jesus: Someone to Accept
Faith Is Consent

On the following days as John stood there again with two of his disciples, Jesus passed, and John stared hard at him and said, "Look, there is the lamb of God." Hearing this, the two disciples followed Jesus. Jesus turned round, saw them following and said: "What do you want?" They answered, "Rabbi" —which means Teacher—where do you live?" "Come and see" he replied; so they went and saw where he lived, and stayed with him the rest of that day. It was about the tenth hour.

One of these two who became followers of Jesus after hearing what John had said was Andrew, the brother of Simon Peter. Early next morning, Andrew met his brother and said to him, "We have found the Messiah—which means the Christ—and he took Simon to Jesus. Jesus looked hard at him and said, "You are Simon son of John; you are to be called Cephas"—meaning Rock.

The next day, after Jesus had decided to leave for Galilee, he met Philip and said: "Follow me." Philip came from the same town, Bethsaida, as Andrew and Peter. Philip found Nathanael and said to him,

"We have found the one about whom the prophets wrote: he is Jesus son of Joseph, from Nazareth." "From Nazareth?" said Nathanael. "Can anything good come from that place?" "Come and see" replied Philip. When Jesus saw Nathanael coming he said of him, "There is an Israelite who deserves the name, incapable of deceit." "How do you know me?" said Nathanael. "Before Philip came to call you," said Jesus, "I saw you under the fig tree." Nathanael answered, "Rabbi, you are the Son of God, you are the King of Israel." Jesus replied, "You believe that just because I said: I saw you under the fig tree. You will see greater things than that." And then he added, "I tell you most solemnly, you will see heaven laid open and, above the Son of Man, the angels of God ascending and descending." (John 1:35–51).

The Ferryman

On the road of faith, Christ is seen as someone who *calls*. On the road where Christ calls the first apostles, the master is depicted as someone who *passes* and the disciple as someone who *stares* after him. Jesus is present, but as the Passerby. John the Evangelist notes that John the Baptist stared hard at Jesus, who was passing. This movement of a disciple who stares at the figure of the master who is passing illustrates one of the basic attitudes of faith.

Staring presupposes a pause, a hesitation, which we have discussed in regard to the disciples of Emmaus. It means getting out of oneself. The one who stares at the other has really already become part of the other.

Passing: But Jesus is actually more of a ferryman than a passerby. And when we hear the word *ferryman* we think of crossing a body of water. This is a baptismal image. Jesus has us cross the sea of life with him just as God led the Israelites across the Red Sea. He *inter-venes*, that is, he "comes between." Not conspicuously. Quite the opposite. In fact, Jesus attracts us by his silence.

• Profiting from an Example

Let's look through the Gospel and glean a few of Christ's sayings, so that we might learn by his example.

Scene One:
What do you want?

Jesus "turned round," says the Gospel. Indeed, Jesus does not just let things go. If he starts something, he always sees where it leads. As in many cases, with the blind man of Jericho, for instance, God begins the dialogues when man takes the first step. Thus, Jesus often asks those who follow him: "What are you waiting for?" Faith is a kind of waiting. Our era is highly sensitive to the right moment; to the favorable conditions we must have so that people may hear the Word. This respect for the propagation of faith, for the soil in which faith grows, for the climate in which it flourishes, is certainly one of the positive things in present-day evangelization.

If we let the pendulum swing too far in one direction we may lose the benefits we've gained. Although the church for centuries may have paid too little attention to the conditions people lived in all the while preaching the Word, our era tends to give top priority to the *prerequisites of faith*. Yet, by waiting for favorable conditions to proclaim Jesus Christ, one risks waiting too long. Jesus himself doesn't seem to have waited until everything was in perfect order in Israel before proclaiming his message. The political situation (the Roman occupation), the social situation (great division between rich and poor and great need on the part of the poor), the religious situation the (formalism of the Pharisees)—none of these factors made evangelizing easy.

Nevertheless, Christ was not afraid to give the sermon on the Bread of Life, which made people call him crazy: "He who comes to me will never be hungry.... Anyone who does eat my flesh ... I shall raise him up" (John 6:35,54). It seems unlikely that today's Christians run much risk of being called wide-eyed madmen. It does seem, therefore, that we would be wise to simply proclaim the Word rather than waiting for just the right "official" moment to do so. In the throes of political struggle, for instance, isn't it essential to think not only about the hopes and expectations the people are able to put into words, but also about those profound aspirations that they themselves may not yet know how to express?

Do you still feel like announcing to the world at large that God loves madness? It's all to the good, I suppose, that Christians have the same slogans of peace and justice that are chalked on walls and printed on protest posters by political activists and deseminated in the media during national political campaigns. Christians might well give some thought to how they might announce to the world "Christ has died, Christ has risen ... "—announce it in the midst of conflicts that all people must resolve in order to bring about peace and justice in the terms that Christ spoke of them.

What are you waiting for? A social system favorable to the Kingdom or even the Kingdom itself? It is indeed true that for generations many Christians chose to ignore the human condition of their fellow Christians—the people of the Kingdom—often falling into angelism and other philosophical and theological dodges to excuse it. But we ought to have learned from the errors of the past. We must never forget the Kingdom and God's people. If we evade or forget it, we open the door to a kind of new messianism, that is, the raising up of an earthly leader or leaders "for the good of the cause." We can already spot the danger signals when we find political leaders and groups taking up the "Christian" standard when it fits their political need: "Our values are Christian values...." Messianism has always been a temptation to people. What it means is the death of God.

The true waiting for the faith revealed in the Gospel springs from the *desire* for God. A person who does not hunger for love has nothing to expect of God. Christ's question, "What do you want?", is an appeal to this hunger. The disciples must express their desire. But we can't head in the right direction—toward God—if we don't find someone to show us the way. The disciples found Jesus because John the Baptist was there to show them the way. And they found God because Christ turned around, turned *them* around. Jesus' reply to the disciples is nothing less than an invitation to take the right road and to let their hearts be turned: "Come and see...." They go. They see. They stay. This tale about the first disciples has something of the story of the disciples of Emmaus in it. "They were walking along the road. They saw Christ. They stayed with him that day."

> *Scene Two:*
> *What do you hear?*

Here is the way the disciples were brought to their Master. It was Andrew who first heard John's words, saw the road he had to follow, and proclaimed of Jesus: "We have found the Messiah!" Andrew, full of the joy of his discovery, took Peter to Jesus. Jesus said nothing. Then looked at Peter. With one look, Jesus possessed Peter completely: "You are Simon son of John; you are to be called Cephas— meaning Rock." (*Petrus*, or *Peter*, is the Latin word for *rock*.) He revealed to him who he was: the same and altogether different; Simon son of John, and Cephas, "stone" or "rock." Jesus didn't tell him "follow me," as he did Philip. Thus it is not written, as about the other disciples, that Peter *followed* Christ. God does not call upon everyone in the same way. Christ's gaze cut Peter to the quick. The look in his eye carried both the call and the answer. God speaks with his eyes and does not ask to be answered with words. When God looks, it is our job to see. When God speaks, it is our job to hear.

Scene Three:
What do you see?

God's call passed through Christ's other followers. Thus, Philip made himself Christ's spokesman for Nathanael. Jesus' words "come and see" were repeated by Philip. But Nathanael didn't say "yes" right away. He asked to *see*: "Can anything good come from Nazareth?", he asked rhetorically. Jesus appreciated this kind of resistance. It showed common sense. Jesus then told Nathanael that he saw him as he passed under the fig tree. This telling detail, this tangible evidence of God's concern for humans, was what made ultimate sense to Nathanael. He found, in this simple revelation, a sign of God's truth. Jesus also showed Nathanael what depth lay beneath his simple revelation "I tell you most solemnly, you will see heaven laid open and, above the Son of Man, the angels of God ascending and descending." While waiting for this happy vision, what do you see? Perhaps those huge paving stones that block the road.

• Huge Paving Stones

Yes indeed, a certain number of difficulties obstruct the hearts of seekers. The trick is not to eliminate these difficulties, but, on the contrary, to look at them point-blank and situate them.

The Revelation

The most massive obstacle is *God as the Word*. God, in revealing himself, has the first word. He decides to make himself known. In fact, with this initiative, he does indeed have the last word. His word is incontestable. The man who seeks God is not forced to appreciate the fact thateverything appears as a "Word of the Gospel." He can assume that the revelation is a trap. Why? Because he is obliged to accept the revelation as a *petitio principii*, or as begging the question. To accept the fact that God reveals himself presumes believing in him. One could think that for Christianity, revelation is a royal road to God. If God himself says who he is, this ought to facilitate the knowledge that we can have of him. Indeed, it's sometimes a handicap. This handicap might diminish if we viewed the Word of God not as something coming from outside, but as a seed that God has deposited in us, all, as a gift.

Quite often we have an extrinsic notion of the Word of God. Many people fancy that God speaks from the outside, as though he were alien to human life. His word is perceived as a meteorite plunging from the sky. Yet the Word of God is not a body alien to human life. If you are seeking, then God must be already talking to you. The Word of God is not a body of information about God, but a guide to reading life, a guide in the light of which we decipher what we are seeking. Recalling this inwardness of the Word does not eliminate the difficulty of the primacy of the Revelation. In fact, one must already be taking the road of faith so that the Word of God may be light. The Word of God is illuminating only for the person who agrees to be converted by it.

One must already have found the road in order to begin seeking. This is Pascal's paradox: "You would not be seeking me if you had not already found me." Such paradox is very nice; but it is precisely what a certain number of seekers reject. They do not want to be duped. Hence, we must understand why man is asked to surrender to the Word of God: it is the Word of Love. To love the Other, one must first believe in him. Believe him on faith, take him at his word. Believing means accepting God as he gives himself.

Believing means consenting to the Word of God, means giving your word as a human being.

The Church
Far more than the *a priori* fact of the Revelation, which is really an intellectual problem, the institution of the church itself can be a great stumbling block to people of goodwill seeking Christ. Roman Catholics the world over are familiar with the usual criticisms of their institutional church: the wealth of the Vatican, the church's historic compromises with the political establishments of the world, etc. But the real problems come on a much simpler and far more serious level. Like it or not, people judge other people and institutions by what they see. They judge the church and Christianity by what they see of priests. After all, priests are the most obvious representatives of the institution. We go to them to be married, to be baptised, to receive communion, to be buried. We expect them to be intensely interested in us and our problems and our requests for their services. But more often than not they seem more interested, to give them the benefit of the doubt, in the more rarified strata of the theological and spiritual worlds and little concerned with our daily needs. And they, the priests, suspect that the average person does not begin to understand the sacraments which they are the agents of dispensing.

Well, the truth is that many people do not understand the sacraments, do not see them as meeting them where they are. And as to the institution of the church, it may call itself the sign of salvation, but the average person in the street probably finds it difficult to see it as such. The real danger is that the church may end by being and making no sign at all. If people perceive priests as being intransigent and the church's concern with the fine points of dogma as petty, then the church will fail in its sincere desire to be

open and receptive to the people of God. On the road of
faith, this kind of misunderstanding, these missed opportu-
nities on both sides, present an enormous dilemma.

A Series of Roadblocks

What are the other obstacles to faith? Roadblocks of
all sorts:

Culture shock. It is certain, for instance, that the techno-
logical or scientific intellects are not to be found struggling
with the problems posed by Christian theology. This fact
was faced generations ago.

Psychological conditionings. Faith requires a certain human equilibrium. How many men, how many women
manage to free themselves from their more or less conscious
inhibitions! How many of them are able to arrive at a
meaningful image of God—not an obvious and unacceptable caricature. How many men, how many women approach God aggressively, projecting onto him their refusal
or outright inability to accept themselves! Plainly, one cannot accept God without accepting oneself. In seeking God,
people are searching out themselves. There's nothing strange
about this. God himself came to seek man *by becoming
man.* However, during this human quest for God, there
comes a moment when a person discovers that he or she can
find himself or herself all the more effectively if, according
to the Gospel, one is willing to lose one's life—that is pass
from egocentrism to theocentrism. To understand the sense
of this passage, one must have already covered a good distance of the road. However, many, many people can't even
begin the journey toward God because the language of faith
seems totally alien to what they are and to what they do. A
person trapped in the web of daily life is hundred of miles
removed from the traditional language of faith. So what
can one say? That faith is a matter of temperament? Of hor-
mones? Of mental processes? A matter of education, of en-

vironment, of chance? Not really—not in theory; not in practice. Then why is true faith so rare?

The polarization of morality. How many men, how many women live, as the phrase goes, in an "irregular situation"! More or less polarized by a sexual morality that preoccupies and swallows whole their sense of religious awareness, they believe they're outside the world of any faith they ever heard about. Although our era claims to be very liberated about sex, morality remains a hidden obstacle to faith, quietly tripping up any number of people. The human sexual condition, for better or worse, weighs very heavily on the scales of faith.

The Great Objections:
Evil, Suffering

The suffering of someone who is truly, deeply suffering is infinitely worthy of respect. This provides ample cause for not believing there is any reason weighty enough to allow us to avoid even the small talk of other people about suffering, talk that on the surface may seem petty to us. Nevertheless, we must admit that at times the discussion of monumental suffering may lead to sheer romanticism. An impressive topic of discussion. What Camus says in *The Plague* about the death of innocent children is staggering: but at times it has been used as something to feed the revolt of late adolescents who don't have any experience of suffering firsthand.

Yet when you've shared the silence of people broken by sorrow, and when you've reached the maturity that comes with plumbing the depths of your own deepest pain, you are less apt to be impressed by self-conscious, public do-gooders who love to be "horrified" at the suffering of others if it provides a fashionable cause for them to take up. No matter how real an obstacle to belief genuine suffering may represent, it can be used by the best of us as an easy, hypocritical way out. "I can't believe because a just God wouldn't allow suffering like that!" How often have you heard that remark?

I know people who are prevented from believing by the suffering of the world—but their awareness doesn't keep them from living it up! Why don't they just say: "I don't believe because I don't feel like believing, because I can't believe, because I can't accept a God who makes people live like dogs!"

Live like dogs. Yes, that's certainly true for many people. Why this natural inequality among people? Why are there people born without talent and intelligence who are forced to do the lowliest tasks all their lives? Why are there other people who always have everything: health, beauty, intelligence, money? Why are some lives handicapped from birth? Why can a meaningless automobile accident maim a decent person and destroy his life plans? Why are there so many people whose daily lives are disconnected—they seem like sleepwalkers moving through an endless vaccum? We Christians should not assume that because Revelation has the *first word* in the person of Jesus, the Word of God, that we must always have the last word on everything. There's nothing shameful about saying: "God knows, I don't!" After all, Jesus didn't give all that many direct, pat answers in the Gospel. So then, let's ask questions. As the great French thinker and writer André Malraux has said: "The civilization of affirmation is over.... This is the civilization of questions." To say it more simply: "The time of dogmatism is over. This is the time of questioning."

· **Such Is Life . . .**
In Black and in Color

After looking at the chief obstacles to faith—whether on God's side with the Revelation and his church, or on man's side with his questions about the ways of God—one must ultimately say: "What can you do, that's life!" And for most people, life itself is an obstacle to faith, either because of its harshness or because of its pleasant meaninglessness.

The weight of the humdrum is crushing. For too much of the year, you leave for work in the morning—it's dark out; you come home in the evening—it's dark out. Not in summer, you say—but for most people, life is an endless winter. Life is a dark business. What dead, zombie-like expressions the people have in the subway! To live without living—that seems to be the fate of the great multitude of people. Dull work in offices with stale air. We are often choked by the smog of disgust in our working lives, and at night when we come home there is the noise of discontent, quarrels, and tension. There is no rest. Life is filled with the infection of illness, with the fear of losing your job, with the wasting fever of pointless love affairs, with the desperation of the teeming almost subhuman masses living or existing in the burrows of slums and shantytowns. One wonders how faith can breathe in these vacant lots of humanity. Doesn't this inhuman life we all share kill faith?

Life, you will say, is not quite as black as I have painted it. Granted, there's love, there are plans that work out, creations that come to fruition. Joy. A child. All the beautiful things. Yes, thank goodness, happiness does exist, too. The world can be wonderful, and life can be a joyous Canticle. And even in winter, when it's cold, you can see crystal dew—turned to frost, of course, but white with hope! So, you have to wonder. Does this attractive catalog mean that the chances for faith developing fully are stronger if one has at least something of the good life? But there is a dark side to comfort. Think about these characteristics of the comfortable: the unconcern of people "without problems," the frequent blindness of those who have managed to reach even the outer edges of faith, the insolence of the rich, the breeziness of parvenus, the insensitivity of the theoretically sensitive. Given all of these factors, the "bed of roses" doesn't seem to make it any easier for faith to blossom.

And we have to think about contradictions. We know it is far too simplistic to infer that faith is possible or impossible depending on how hard or easy life is—whatever interpretation we put on the spiritual benefits and liabilities of the hard or the easy life. We all know people whose lives are very difficult and who live in true, complete faith. Likewise, we all know people whose lives are serene, who also live in complete faith. If the obstacles inherent in God and in humans lead us back to life, then life itself leads us to the human heart. The conditioning factors of human life determine faith. But on a deeper level, the thing that makes faith possible or impossible is the human heart itself.

Troubled Waters

Human beings are innately lazy. What God asks of us is contrary to our *natural* inclination. On the level of the great goals—peace, justice, brotherhood, truth, freedom— we are caught up in the awesomeness of Revelation which alone seems able to fulfill these ideals for us. But God's Revelation has to do with the greatest things that people can aspire too. On the level of our petty, day-to-day aspirations, what really inspires us? We want to succeed. But what does that mean? What else do we hope to realize in our work? What else do we want in our work? To get a raise? Why a raise? To raise what raises our raises. Enjoyment: a comfortable place to live, a new car so that we can then get another new car after our new car is no longer so new.

Everything that our day-to-day life offers seems, in some ways, to go against the ideals that God reveals to us in the Beatitudes: "Blessed are the poor! He who wishes to be my disciple must take up his cross! Renounce even his own life!" The revelation of ordinary life seems to be a counter-revelation to the great Revelation of God. Then what about faith? Faith is to accept the fact that God has something more and different to offer us than our individual portion of the fruits of the earth. We are worth more than what we ever succeed in being. Believing is consenting to be saved. It means calling by its real name the tare or weed that chokes the wheat: sin. Only faith can reveal the part that sin plays in our lives and in our refusal to accept God. Sin itself is to a large extent the major obstacle to faith. But not everything is settled by recognizing sin.

A Field of Wheat in a Seed of Tare

In the face of all these obstacles, especially that of evil, the only response we have is Jesus Christ. Jesus Christ brought one answer: *himself.* God did not argue. God has no arguments. God was at the end of all arguments: the cross! God is not *above* suffering. That is his strength. It's quite easy, in a way, to reject a God who tolerates suffering. But we also know that God doesn't deceive us. He doesn't try to make us believe that suffering is not suffering. Rather than resorting to rhetoric, God did everything he could. Isn't it amazing to think of Almighty God "doing what he can?" God cannot do more than God. Let us have the honesty of the man who has little to say, and the courage of the man who chooses to live. Such is the faith that moves mountains.

Let's not try to justify the unjustifiable. But at the same time, let's not say that the existence of the unjustifiable justifies our rejection of God. Accepting God as he is means, first of all, looking beyond the un-understandable, unresolvable debate about mutual wrongs in the timeless relationship of God to humankind.

We have moved far afield since our first encounter with the disciples. And yet, in the twisting and turning of our journey of exploration, we have followed in their footsteps, and tried to see God, who crosses quietly through the darkness and obscurity of our lives. We have found man caught in the fabric of life. Let us try to remember the truths the disciples themselves taught us.

We cannot find God if we do not hunger for him. The disciples saw Jesus because they were waiting for Jesus. The man who expects nothing has nothing to expect of God. The man who does not hope for God cannot find him. Faith is promise: the seed of *hoping*, which becomes the seed of Hope.

> God be praised!
> When the undergrowth invades
> The field of our life,
> Hope can still arise,
>
> for you are the Lord
> the only one who can see
> a field of wheat
> in a seed of tare.

5

Jesus: Someone Who Engages You

Faith Is Constancy

Now as he drew near to Jericho there was a blind man sitting at the side of the road begging. When he heard the crowd going past he asked what it was all about, and they told him that Jesus the Nazarene was passing by. So he called out, "Jesus, the son of David, have pity on me." The people in front scolded him and told him to keep quiet, but he shouted all the louder, "Son of David, have pity on me." Jesus stopped and ordered them to bring the man to him, and when he came up, asked him, "What do you want me to do for you?" "Sir," he replied, "Let me see again." Jesus said to him, "Receive your sight. Your faith has saved you." And instantly his sight returned and he followed him praising God, and all the people who saw it gave praise to God for what had happened. (Luke 18:35–43)

Theater of Life, Mystery of Faith

On the road of faith, Christ is the light that illuminates every person. "The light shines in the darkness." Is that why Christ likes to reveal himself through blind people?

With the blind man of Jerusalem—the one who was blind from birth—we were in a courtroom. Attending a judgment. With the blind man of Jericho, we are in an open-air theater. Attending a mystery. The theater of life. The mystery of faith. The scenario is the same as in most stories about a cure. We find the same characters: Jesus, the sick man, the disciples, the crowd. The plot is more or less the same: The man calls; Jesus replies. But God is in a different dimension than that in which the question is asked. He does not answer the question at its own level. He answers what lies at the heart of it and what lies beyond it: "Go, your faith has saved you." The denouement, as expected, runs according to the usual clichés: everyone is happy and they say that Jesus is extraordinary!

This tale of the blind man of Jericho is presented by the evangelists in several forms. I don't know if Saint Matthew was seeing double (you can see for yourself: 20:29–34), but he saw *two* blind men! Not that it matters, for it's the same story, give or take a few details. Mark and Matthew put this episode at the place where they left Jericho. Luke says it happened at the gate of the town: "As Jesus was approaching Jericho...." The evangelists don't have exactly the same notion of unity of space and time. But so what? The essence of the story is the same. On the other hand, the three evangelists agree on the conclusion: the blind man follows Jesus.

· **The Sorrow and the Pity**
   The Mob

The crowd is the blind self.

The crowd is what's inside us. It is *we, ourselves*. It's that which constitutes us. It is the "pile of secrets" that Malraux talks about. It inhabits us. It is the "inexhaustible self" that the great poet Paul Valéry speaks of: the crowd of lovely desires that lives in our hearts. Plans, dreams, and reminiscences, the hope for a world in which humans would be human for humans. The crowd is also the sad self wrinkled by the grief and tears of the night. Ultimately, it is the hateful self, the self that Pascal speaks of: rejection, egoism, obstinacy, disloyalty—in a word, everything that knocks us off the road to our salvation. Aren't these things sin: blinding oneself, fooling others and thereby oneself (for in final analysis, one fools only oneself), and then, in the end, discovering that one has lost oneself completely? Let's not look very far afield for the blind man. He's right here, within us; and all the while, we are exiled outside ourselves.

The crowd, it's the others.

For my neighbor: "others" means me. I am one of the others, those people out there. The crowd immediately surrounding me is, first of all, the small group of people one knows well, of intimates whom we often see and yet don't see. The circle of near and dear among whom one moves but from whom one remains apart, mystery never seeing inside them. Thus, not infrequently, a man may leave his brother to spend his whole life by the side of the road, in his night and isolation. Thus, for one's wife or husband, one's brother, children, or friend, one is the anonymous crowd oneself. The teeming crowd. The crowd that has always been blind. Jesus knew the crowd. I believe that he loved the crowd and that he was afraid of it. He loved feeling physically caught in this nameless solidarity with others. Knowing you're like the others and not like the others. Jesus bathed in the crowd. He got lost in the crowd. In the great circuses that religious pilgrimages often were in his time! The crowd giving an ovation: the miracle of the loaves and fishes. The applauding crowd: the surge of branches on Palm Sunday. The hooting crowd: the Good Friday mob. Jesus pitied the crowd; all the more so since he knew profoundly each person in it.

The Prompter's Part

There is a blind man. Saint Mark calls him Bartimaeus (the son of Timaeus). Bartimaeus cries out: "Have pity on me!" Nowadays, pity is not considered a noble sentiment. Too many people remember what Nietzsche had to say about Christians who, he believed, fled life and took refuge in pity. The atheistic criticism of pity is also severe—it contributes to alienation, they say. It would indeed be alienation if man, resigning himself to his misery, expected everything of a condescending God who would agree to pity him. Pity can also be scornful. There is a haughty way of bending down, supposedly out of love, over the "poor wretch." This kind of pity is insulting.

However, in the Bible, pity is the face assumed by God's love when God takes human misery to heart. It is mercy. A noble thing. Confronted with so much distress—death, separation—and so many impasses in which human love is at the end of its tether, a Christian can cry out to God in all truth: "Lord, take pity!" Confronted with so much misery, when the poverty of men becomes, in Jesus Christ, the very poverty of the Son of Man, then God's pity is God's honor. The Christian can say without shame: "Lord, take pity!" And when dignity and honor mingle with silent tears, then, if pity bursts forth like a cry of hope, can one blame a blind man for crying out: "Pity!"?

In his night, the blind man hears the crowd scolding, just as one hears the ocean behind a dune. He calls all the more loudly because he can't see. He would like to know; he would like to see what he has never seen. He asks. He wonders what that noise means. Mark says that "they" inform the blind man that Jesus is passing. Who are "they"? Men of goodwill, perhaps, who sense that the blind man may be in luck if he is there when the Lord passes by. But there are also in the crowd embittered souls who refuse to hear anything. Bartimaeus is scolded by them for shouting, so he shouts all the more loudly. He is told quite simply, "Shut up!" It's not that the crowd is necessarily nasty—but what can you do? They have their problems too. They too are by the side of the road. Do they see more clearly? Poor themselves, do they realize they're humiliating Bartimaeus? Unfortunately, the poor know what they're doing when they humiliate him: they're harsher than the rich man would dream of being. And in the midst of all this—Christ appears. We now have to read the story in Saint Mark (10:46–52).

In order to make the others recognize him, Christ waits for them to show themselves first. Do you notice? Jesus does not address the blind man directly. He signals to the crowd; he orders them to call Bartimaeus. "Call him!" he says. Since the others have told the blind man of Christ's coming even before the cure takes place, the first miracle is performed: Bartimaeus (notes Saint Mark), still blind, "dropping his cloak, starts to leap." The progress of faith presupposes dropping a certain number of old habits that cling to us. The blind man, now freed of his old ways, begins to run. Have you ever seen a blind man running, leaping? Yes, that's the miracle. Faith lends wings. Before meeting Christ, before being cured, Bartimaeus was still able to believe in others, to believe what they told him was about to happen. Believing in man, he could believe in God. Basically, we human beings don't, by instinct, want to rely on or need other people. And yet Christ teaches us that we can't do without others, because he sometimes comes to us through others. Other people have an irreplaceable role in meetings with Christ. When you don't know what to say, what to do, others play the role of prompter. The prompter is unobtrusive. He does not play an actor's part: with a word, he allows the other to find himself again and play his part. Now Bartimaeus has *been* prompted, he has come to the place where he has been told he will find Christ. And Christ does not ask the crowd what Bartimaeus wants; he speaks to the blind man directly.

Replying

"What do you want me to do for you?" The question may seem preposterous, insolent. What do you expect a blind man to ask for if not to see? The real author of this scenario, the Holy Spirit, obviously knows that sight is all the blind man expects. The Spirit will now be prompting Christ—the leading actor—giving him the line that will be a good reply to the blind man. He acts as he did with the woman of Samaria and with so many other people: Christ's question (he who knows everything) evinces the freedom of the man who calls upon him. The Gospel notes that Christ asks his question when he is *near* the blind man; and the story specifies at the beginning: "As Jesus drew near to Jericho there was a blind man sitting at the side of the road begging." Jericho! God keeps approaching our world, where we are protected, closed in by walls, each of us like a fortified city. God circles our walls. He asks us to level the walls of our prejudices and open the gates to let him in. His revelation of himself is like the goddess Aurora's offering to the day in Roman mythology. Being loyal to light means departing in mist and finding that indeed the sun is already out as faith told us it should be.

This is the whole dynamics of faith understood as the gift of God, who calls, and the welcoming answer by humans, who respond as they are able. God loves us first. He precedes us. He approaches. He signals the departure, but it is up to us to set out. The father of the prodigal son went to meet his boy, but it was the son who had first decided to set out towards his father. The father did not go looking for him. Christ does not go looking for the blind man. The father believed his son would come down the road, but it was the son who took the first step. Like the father of the prodigal son, God's arms are open to us, but that's all he can do. God is no huckster. He's not trying to hawk his goods, to sell faith at any price. He seeks us for our sake: "What do you want me to do for *you*?" Jesus doesn't say: "What do you want me to do to make you a believer?" The faith that saves is the faith that illuminates us and allows us to know about ourselves. Being faithful to God is being faithful to oneself. One can, of course, take the wrong road, make a mistake, find oneself lost in the dark and shout for help. Believing means knowing that God's word can never deceive; and it means admitting that we *can* deceive and even blind ourselves! Judging by the way Jesus speaks against the Pharisees, we can see that God is enraged by those who blind themselves. To fool God deliberately, to fool others, to fool oneself knowingly—don't these acts constitute the troubling sin against the Holy Spirit that is labeled as being "without forgiveness" and that seems to be the special crime of the fearful yet tragic being who refuses the light: the Prince of Darkness?

All the People Who Saw It

Faith saved the blind man. Jesus said so. Who else but Jesus could have said so? Do you realize the full meaning of these words? The same Jesus who told the paralyzed man: "Go, your sins are forgiven" declares peremptorily, in this case, "Go, your faith has saved you." Which is more difficult, more extraordinary for Jesus to say: "Go, your faith has saved you" or "Go, your sins are forgiven"? They both boil down to the same thing. It is for saying, "Go, your sins are forgiven" that Jesus becomes suspect in the eyes of the Pharisees and is accused of blasphemy by them; for God alone can forgive sins. Likewise, God alone can authenticate a person's faith. Thus, discreetly, indirectly, Jesus has indicated that he is, if not the Son of God, then at least "of God."

To our eyes, Bartimaeus and Jesus are far from being on the same plane. Bartimaeus has only one thing on his mind: to recover his eyesight. He addresses Jesus, knowing he has nothing to lose. Isn't this Jesus renowned as a healer? What is this man's faith? Superstition? I would say: "blind confidence." But even confidence needs to be enlightened, evangelized, saved. Confidence alone is never enough; but it may be the first step towards faith. To suspect blind confidence on the grounds that it is often ambiguous and self-seeking may be condemning a person to stay put and never go any further.

No doubt, in the lives of many people faith is understood to mean the simple belief that God will say: "Go, your faith has saved." If Jesus were a member of a consistory of the church, he would no doubt be forced to resign. In an era in which we make a subtle distinction between religion and faith, in which we analyze the purity of motives in those who ask for sacraments, this simple, direct approach of Christ's would shock many people! Jesus' attitude reminds us that a person's innermost secret will always elude us. When people come and request a mass for a reason different from the mass's reason, a baptism for a reason different from the baptism's reason, a blessing for a reason different from that which God's blessing represents, then they are no doubt coming as blind men, as beggars, like Bartimaeus. They come to shout things that they do not yet know how to formulate according to criteria they have not yet found. They come to knock at the door of a church that calls itself a "servant" and "poor." What do they find? Militants, priests, ministers, nuns who sometimes say: "Shut up and be grateful!", by way of welcoming poeple into a church that we would ideally like open, clean, neat, and well swept. We are so anxious to see a true and, all the while, orderly church, that we are virtually paralyzed when we have to receive true paupers. And paupers not just in terms of material wealth; paupers who are so naive and impoverished in spiritual book-learning that they do not understand our refined pastoral categories and on the occasion of a wedding or a funeral might dare to beg for a bit of human warmth, a sign of hope through a sacrament that, for us the enlightened, may represent something different from what paupers know about or can understand. We like paupers when they fit into our classifications. But once they threaten to impoverish our favorite religious concepts —well that's another matter! The church is willing to *call* itself poor. But, through us all, does the church and do all of us, the faithful, agree to be "impoverished" by the poor in the image it reflects?

I do not intend to inhibit or deny the worth of the efforts people make towards an intelligent and demanding pastoral image for the church. Quite the opposite: I just think we need to remember that the people by the roadside, those known as marginal, may need to hear one day in their lives: "What do you want me to do for you? Simply *for you*." Isn't it possible that the light of faith could well be revealed to them through this question? The light that impels us to see clearly and follow Jesus. Bartimaeus the marginal man; "... instantly his sight returned," says Saint Luke, "and he followed him praising God." Saint Mark says more simply: "followed after Jesus."

All's well that ends well. The curtain drops amid thunderous applause. "And all the people who saw it gave praise to God for what happened." Bartimaeus has become a disciple! Wicked tongues can always say that there was no great merit in following Christ on the spot. Bartimaeus lived on little or nothing, he had no wife or children, no responsibilities. But it doesn't say that he, too, didn't have to bear his cross in order to follow Christ. And just what does it mean to follow Christ? Let us take time to think about what the word *follow* means in the Gospel sense, in order to pinpoint what *faithfulness* means when we speak of faith as a life of following Christ.

• Going After
Going Well with Christ

Follow is a key word in the Gospel. It is also a key word in life: "Come right in. Follow me." We hear it every day. It's the sort of thing a dentist says when he asks you into his office. Colloquially, the word *follow* can evoke a passive attitude. Most likely because the person who follows is in back, behind the one who leads. To illustrate this one might draw on animal imagery: "He follows me like a little dog"; "Follow the ox." The Christian, indeed, is sometimes reproached for following like a sheep.

Jesus himself teaches us that to "follow behind" is not necessarily the same thing as being "in tow." A certain number of current expressions indicate as much. Have you ever seen the farmer's wife lead the cows to pasture? And what about the shepherd? How often is he forced to lead his sheep by switching along the last ewe who is lagging behind? And what does a physician do when he "follows up" on the condition of a patient? Wait for the disease to vanish as though by magic? Quite the contrary. He provides the "patient" with effective care, treatment, surveillance. Thus, *to follow* is, in a certain sense, *to precede*. Following indicates a dynamic movement.

To follow Christ is, first of all, to recognize God, who comes to man in the guise of a shepherd. As such, the guide in this case both leads the way and brings up the rear.

To follow Christ is thus to acknowledge that God pursues us with his love, both preceding and following us in everything we do.

In our path toward God, it doesn't matter whether we're at the head of the line or at the tail end. It doesn't matter whether we're sitting at the roadside like the blind man of Jericho or walking down the center of the road, like the disciples of Emmaus. The essential thing is to "go well" with Christ.

To follow Christ is to walk with him as one would walk with a favorite companion. Following in his footsteps is not servile. Christ allows his disciple a full initiative to make the first move. Thus, Bartimaeus, who barely knows Jesus, goes out to meet God. Jesus then tells him: "Come!" This verb explodes like an interjection. In the Gospels, this active monosyllable "Come!" very often precedes "Follow me!" as though to mark the quickening of spirit that triggers the disciple's decision to follow. One doesn't *submit* to following Christ. One *takes* the lead in order to follow him.

Every Baptized Person Is a Disciple

On this road of life which one walks with the Risen Lord, Jesus is very engaging. Engaging, first of all, because his words promise marvels. "If someone is thirsty, let him come to me, rivers of living water will spurt forth in him as an inexhaustible wellspring of life! If someone is hungry, let him come to me, he will be sated for life!" Engaging, because words like these make you want to taste promise of faith. Engaging, because Jesus was the first to "engage" himself, pledge himself, commit himself to humanity. How could God engage himself more completely than by becoming human?

To follow Christ is to recognize God's engagement, his commitment in the lives of men; this means a response, a committing of oneself heart and soul—as Jesus Christ did—to live one's life in God. The Christian's commitment is not one commitment among many. For a baptized person, being committed doesn't mean joining a movement, giving some time to a group, rendering a service. A Christian's commitment is nothing less than the baptized person's total immersion in the life of the Risen Christ. The committed Christian is not just "invested in Christ"; the baptized person has Christ "under his skin!"

To follow Christ is to "live in Christ," as Saint Paul describes it. In this sense, every baptized person is a disciple. To follow Christ is not a demand reserved for a few volunteers caught up in the religious life; it is the fundamental demand of Christianity, revealing to us that the Risen Christ is the path for humankind to follow. Since this baptismal commitment is a lifelong mission for Christians, the call to be a disciple becomes absolute: "Abandon all else."

How can we fit the infinite landscape of the evangelical call within the restricted limits of our human possibilities? Given the frustration inherent in the human inability to ever give a perfect, complete response to Christ's call, how can we prevent the "fire of life" from going out within us? How can we resist the temptation to pare down God's transcendence to our own size?

Prophetic Gestures

Every baptized person is a prophet. A prophet not in the sense of the popular orator who denounces injustice and lectures everyone on the righteous path. But rather, a prophet in the sense of a witness who speaks through a Christian life lived in God. Every Christian is called upon —perhaps once, perhaps several times in his or her life—to perform one or more prophetic acts, acts which, though limited by their humanness, testify to the unlimited range of God's desire. For some, the act may be a major decision, an option in life that irreversibly shapes the future, the adoption of a life style that makes it impossible to accept compromise of the principles on which it is based. Living conditions, social pressure can determine the way we live. "To follow Christ" presupposes freedom, room to breathe. If we are unable to cut free from our familiar moorings we can easily lose track of the fact that we are stagnating in the familiar waters of our home port—and yet, being human, we're perfectly capable of imagining we're living in the fast flowing current and fresh air of the open sea!

"If you want to follow Christ, leave that old tub, which is as old as you, abandon your imprisoning snares, find at least one break in the net to escape to freedom!" This break in life may be a very simple but by no means insignificant gesture. A prophetic gesture is a gesture that *means some-thing*. We honestly desire to follow Christ as far as we're able; we realize how frequently we trip over stones in the road. There is a way to proclaim the reality of this desire and to protest against our inability to carry it out fully: from time to time, do something gratuitous; give away something that you value. We all have objects that we value because they "speak to us" in a special way. It's all right to value them. But don't you feel that in some ways, these material attachments don't quite square with the freedom of a Christian?

"Leave everything!" But the Gospel is really not all or nothing. In the *all of life*, Christ suggests little *nothings* to us. Christ knows how to view those nothings as an all when they express the all of life dedicated to him. He doesn't ask more of us than he has empowered us to give.

Free to Be a Slave

God is not a tyrant. He reveals to us, paradoxically, in the Servant Christ, that "the master is not above the disciple." In proposing an ideal of life above our abilities to reach, Christ is not really placing himself above man. On the contrary, according to the hymn that Paul brings to the Philippians: "Jesus behaved like a man, he humbled himself, taking on the condition of a slave." Becoming human, Jesus calls upon all men to become like God. Here, we must remember the Gospel: "The disciple is not above the master!" Walking behind Christ, in imitation of Christ, means entering the Master's joy. When one admires someone, happiness lies in resembling him. Faith is an imitation of Jesus Christ. "I cannot see the poor Christ," said Charles de Foucauld, "without feeling an urgent need to resemble him." But resemblance does not mean being a carbon copy. Faith is not mimicry. Christ resembles the Father and the Spirit because he always remains what he is: the Son of God. He reveals to us that evangelical submissiveness is an essentially filial attitude. Following Christ as a disciple means living with God as a loving son lives with his father. Only this love can inspire the disciple. The goal is not a literal reproduction of what Jesus went through; it is not a material rerun of what he did. Every individual has to find his or her own way of being faithful. Faith is faithfulness, but not in a moralizing sense. The goal is not so much to succeed in applying the precepts, as it is to cast one's life in the mold of Christ. To follow Christ is to take shape with Christ. Paul does not conceal the fact that this shape is a form of slavery. To fear admitting this to our contemporaries, who are so intent on freedom in every aspect of their lives, means deceiving them about the truth of the Gospel and making trivial the Christian mystery; it means dodging the Resurrection. Not to be bold enough to say that cherishing Christ means cherishing the cross is tantamount—says a tearful Saint Paul—to "behaving as the enemies of the cross of Christ" (Philippians 3:18).

Saint Paul also reveals that this slavery is paradoxically born from freedom, as life is born from death. He says: "Not a slave of any man I have made myself a slave of everyone" (I Corinthians 9:19). Anyone who loves knows that love is enthralling. Parents may be theoretically free in regard to their children, but aren't they all the more enslaved to them the more they love them?

The Christian does not endure slavery as the tyranny of a

master; he is *free to be a slave.* He is free to love him who fetters us to himself in order to free us from our false liberties. Thus, the French spiritual writer Father Pousset explains very clearly what sort of slavery this is: "Christ is Life, beyond the life that is the opposite of death; just as he is freedom beyond the freedom that is the opposite of servitude. And this is shown by his twofold renunciation of freedom and life: human beings reduce it to servitude, but this slave has the power to give his life freely, and he does so. Human beings put him on the cross, and he dies; but from this death, the master of life rises again. Such are the words that manifest what God is: Love."

The Christian is detained, a prisoner. He obtains from God the freedom to love as God loved. In this love, he is free to reject the bondage created by all the delusions and passions of domination, which are very harshly stigmatized by Saint Paul: "They make their bellies into their gods, and they are proudest of something they ought to think shameful; the things they think important are earthly things" (Philippians 3:19). The "Apostle of the gentiles," while pitiless towards servile hedonists, does not scorn the joys of creation. He merely reminds us that the existence of heaven gives earth its dimension of infinity. To follow Christ is thus, ultimately, to walk with him on earth while looking toward heaven. Being faithful to Christ does not mean being free of sin. It means seeing the adventure through, while gazing until the last moment like Saint Peter crucified, "head down, feet up," as legend has it. Isn't this the best possible image of the disicple Peter, the apostle of Hope!

> Lord,
> in his ardor
> Peter cried:
> "Wherever you go
> I will follow you."

He followed you until cockcrow,
His soul in tears, his heart in tatters.
But your Love sang within him.
        You subjugate you seduce
        He followed you until his death
And the death of the cross and the cross of life.

Through the days and through the nights
Let us walk in your direction
Pursue us with your Presence,
So that we then may say to you:
        "Wherever I go
        Lord
        You can follow me."

— 6

Jesus: Someone Filial. God Is Father.

Faith Is Confidence

The Jewish Prayer of Kaddish or Sanctification of the Name.

The Officiant:

And now, may you be exalted and filled with grace, by the power of our Lord who promised that it would be so when he said (Numbers 14:17): "Remember us mercifully, O Eternal One, with your grace, for it endureth forever" (Psalm 25:6).

The Officiant and the Congregation:

- That your mighty Name be magnified and sanctified in the world which was created by your will; and that your Reign be established in our lives and in our days, and in the life of all the house of Israel, now and forever; and let us all say: Amen!
- That your Name be honored forever, and be eternally blessed, celebrated, glorified, honored, magnified and exalted as your Holy Name, blessed be it, and worthy of all blessing, praise, and homage

which can be said on earth; and let us all say:
Amen!
  · That the prayers and supplication of all Israel be
received by their Father who is in heaven; and let
us all say: Amen!
  · That universal peace is granted us from heaven,
and that it be upon us all our lives, and upon all
Israel; and let us say: Amen!
  · That He who established peace on high, grant it to
us and to all Israel, and let us all say: Amen!

A God in General?

God. What is his name? What is he called? *God* is
an abstract word like *man*. When I speak about man with
no article, I mean, human beings in general. When I speak
about God with no article and with a capital *G*, I mean
God in general, the Supreme Being. God is not a general
God. He is universal and particular. He is himself, personally. And not only the Infinite, the Absolute, Perfection, Eternity. When I speak about man in the abstract, I
am referring to the concrete experience of knowing the
human beings that I encounter day after day. When I
speak about God, I can refer to no other god than God
himself. He is unique. I then consult Revelation. But the
Bible is not an encyclopedia about God. It supplies only
the key words, the clues to the unfathomable secrets of
God. It communicates the essence of God, the vital things
about him, which allow us to enter into contact with him
who nevertheless remains Unknown. Hence, it's no use
saying that God is not an idea, but Someone; for most people, God remains an abstraction. And most ordinary people have better things to do than seek a God with no face,
address a God with no address, call to a God with no
name.

• God: The Unknown Father?
Abba and Papa

You will say: It's hard to give God a name. "They" are three in one! The Father. The Son. The Spirit. At least the Son's name is known: Jesus. But Jesus is a first name. When people are part of the same family, they call each other by their first names. People would like to be able to call "God in general" by his first name. But the Old Testament came up with nothing better than a group name for the three persons. "God united" is called Yahweh: "I am that I am." But this is more of a definition than a proper name! The Hebrews, filled with "fear and trembling" before God, would never name him. They called to him by spelling the first letters of the word Adonai. This is an anagram meaning: *Lord.* But *Lord* isn't a proper name. It's more of a title designating God's royal rank as Sovereign Master of the Universe; while the word *Abba* (Father) in Hebrew designates God in his loving existence, in his loving relationship to human beings. When you say "Father" to God, it's a bit like a child saying "Papa" to the man who fathered him. *Abba* and *papa* are the same word. In Hebrew, *Abba* has an emotional nuance that corrects anything cold and anonymous in God's universal fatherhood. Thus, the common noun *father* becomes a proper noun, the name for God when, in faith, one becomes filial in regard to God the Unique Father for all. And one becomes fraternal in regard to all human beings who recognize this universal father.

Fundamentally, believing is recognizing God as one's father. This may appear simple, yet it is not just a matter of course. Nowadays, linking God and the Father sometimes means provoking the deepest sensibilities of young people.

"God Is Dead," But Not the Father . . . .

In the nineteenth century philosophers in Europe proclaimed the death of God. The twentieth century is quite alarmed to find the corpse is moving. The God who was condemned to die was simply not executed. It was not enough for the nineteenth-century thinkers to decree a sentence. And whether we, with our rather watered-down approach to religion and our severely ailing world, like it or not, the corpse is still breathing. In their obstinacy of faith, Christians, without talking about it, are keeping him alive, prolonging his life. It's as though all these unknown, unnamed believers had gotten up a petition from the universe of the ordinary people and thus managed to have him reprieved! Dead and Risen One, this is your victory! It is final and yet the battle isn't over. There are those who are still seeking a grave for God. A black hole. A stone that can't be rolled aside or lifted. The nineteenth-century cried: "God is dead!" Many twentieth-century people are still trying to figure out how to bury him. They think they've found a way. The twentieth century is out to kill the Father. God is dead. But the Father—not yet! And God *is* God the Father. To link God with the Father is a challenge to the younger generation, marked by psychoanalysis and talk about "murdering the father" as a prerequisite for adulthood. This is one of the challenges of faith today. Thus, in order that God may live, this God who's been condemned to death, we must urgently sort out our experiences of human fatherhood, which we risk projecting onto God. If we wish to resurrect God in modern awareness and reconcile him with all the psychological disciplines seeking "profound man," then it's time we dropped all masks and washed all makeup from our fathers' faces. It's time we cleaned up our notions of a father, scoured them with the water of truth. It's time we "demythified" the ideal father. It's time we opened ourselves to the Revelation of God the Father. It's high time. Today is the time of God. And the time of man.

From the Fathers on Earth . . . to the Father in Heaven

"Honor your father and mother so that you may live long." This Mosaic commandment consecrates a universal human feeling: a father, a mother are by nature sacred. In the garden of Creation, fatherhood is at the heart of human joys. How can one help but exalt the love that gives life? Who can list all the joys of being a father: the love continued in another self; the deep tenderness that is reborn in a baby's smile; the love held out to opening arms; the love of a baby's first steps; the love that grows with the child; the tried-and-tested love when the child is no longer a child?

But who can tell me where the Father of Love is to be found? From the ideal Father to real fathers—there's many a slip 'twixt the cup and the lip. One can chide the new generation for being aggressive, narcissistic; but one can't deny its lucidity. Young people are not unaware of the potential for goodness and beauty in fathers and fatherhood. Amid so many broken homes, abandoned children, they quite simply reject the *myth* of the pelican-father sacrificed for his young. Amid so much arrogance camouflaged as pride, so much poor upbringing, so much cowardice fobbed off as closeness, so much egotism, young people reject the myth of the *good father*—as if *good* and *father* were necessarily linked. Young people are repelled at the hypocrisy of a society that exploits the noble sentiment of fatherhood to impose the authority of an established order, while desertion by fathers is everywhere deplored. They reject the image of the father as a disciplinary authority, whom you respect automatically and never "talk back to." They denounce the prostitution of fatherhood—the commercialization of it (Father's Day) and the manipulation of it (using fatherhood symbolically to set up psychological straw men).

In our relationship to God the Father, we are deeply marked by all these seemingly trivial ideas about fathers which have nothing to do with our faith in the *divine fatherhood*. Subconsciously, however, they burden our hearts and alienate our minds. We depend on the "trademark image" of a father as manufactured by the system. But we cannot picture the Heavenly Father by ignoring our notion of earthly fathers. We cannot experience God the Father by disregarding our experience of earthly fathers. So many men and women pray "Our Father" to God without even knowing what they're saying; so many Christians dare not admit to themselves that they cannot accept God as the Father because they have been traumatized by experiences which prevent them from being "sons" or "daughters."

Since faith hinges on a filial relationship with God, it is important to get at the truth about earthly fatherhood; the point is not to discredit the great traditional themes of human paternity, but rather to smash the facades that make them unreal and unacceptable. In this respect, birth control has produced a certain truth. "Responsible" fatherhood is one of the greatest moral strides in our era. Not only does it increase man's power over life, but it also reveals his poverty before the love he is capable of in order to master this power. Fatherhood is aimed at the other, the child; but the father—who is also a husband!—now realizes that he usually begins by loving himself. This innate human egoism keeps us from seeing human paternity ideally.

So, hats off to today's young people who don't fall for glib slogans easily and are liberated enough not to see themselves as outcasts and bad children when they denounce the failings of human paternity, which, ultimately, is never what it should be. A lingering question remains: Will their critical powers make better fathers of *them*?

No One Knows the Father
Human fatherhood originates in God's Fatherhood. Man, created in God's image, to some extent participates in

the mystery of divine fatherhood. Thus, to approach the mystery of God the Father, we cannot avoid analogy; that is, noting the approximate resemblances and essential differences between human experience and the part of God's Revelation that we know. It is not the experience of human fatherhood that helps us discover what divine fatherhood is, but vice versa. God comes first. It is God's fatherhood, fully realized as it is, that reveals the mystery of human fatherhood to us. There is both continuity and discontinuity between our knowledge of earthly fathers and our knowledge of the Heavenly Father. That is why it is so important to guard against applying our human categories to God without careful consideration. Humanly speaking, we can view the father-son relationship in purely chronological terms. The father precedes the child in time. This simple fact has a concrete impact on the father-son relationship; it causes the generation gap we hear about: the power of the father who crushes the child, etc. But in God, this chronological question does not exist. God has no age. The Father as well as the Son are eternal. In the beginning was the Word. The Father always is and has been the Father. The Son is perpetually begotten. He is not created. From these simple viewpoints of time and eternity, we can see that the Father-Son relation in the Trinity is not comparable to that of human beings. God transcendent is a completely different Father. This radical difference is stressed by Jesus in many ways.

First of all, he tells us: "No one knows the father except the son" (Matthew 11:27). No one can know what goes on in God but God himself. And by teaching us the Lord's Prayer, teaching us to say "Our Father," Jesus distinguishes between the relationship uniting him to his Father and our relationship to the Father, which is not on the same level. He pinpoints: "Do not confuse my Father and your Father." The Father whom Jesus sees is the Father that we merely glimpse through the mediation of the Only Begotten Son. "He who sees me sees the Father," says Jesus! A vision of faith.

Just as there is no human time frame in the relationship of the Father and the Son in God, so in faith, there is no chronology, no movement from day to night. Faith is a strange blend of dawn and dusk in our hearts, so that in our search for God we never know whether it is morning or evening. God remains the unknown, but in every human being, every day, his light rises. In other words, we can perceive something of this "unknown Father," because we know that the Spirit, in our heart of hearts, knows the Father and knows us. And the Spirit, who knows the Father, and He, who knows humans, knows that beyond our strivings and stirrings we have a deep, unchangeable desire "to know God as we are known by him." We humans have a wild dream of finally being able to apply a proper noun, a name, to love. This is when the Spirit, clamoring for God, cries out: "Abba, Father!" If we open the doors of our innermost beings, we can see the brightness that made an old man about to receive the last rites say: "I'm dying to see Him!"

· Like Father, Like Son . . .
Jesus, the Image of His Father . . .

As recorded in the four Gospels, especially in Saint John, Jesus' statements about his Father are always grave and sententious. But Jesus was not just solemn! He must have had relaxed conversations with his apostles and given free and spontaneous vent to his feelings. The conversation must have been going at a good pace the day that Philip— perhaps upset by Jesus' failure to come to the point—told him, "Let us see the Father and then we shall be satisfied" (John 14:8). That's enough for us, it means: "We'll be happy!" Or perhaps, simply, "You always keep saying the same thing!"

> "I am in the Father, and the Father is in me.
> It is the Father, living in me,
> who is doing this work"
>
> (John 14:10)

> "If you know me,
> You know my Father too."
> (John 14:7)

This insistence by Jesus, who does not hesitate to repeat the same thing thirty-six times, always in a slightly different way, not only shows the intense unity of the Father and the Son; it also reveals that this unity constitutes the Being of God, a Being in a relationship: the Father with the Son in the same Spirit.

This unity is made of love: "The world must be brought to know that I love the Father," says Jesus (John 14:31). How moving to hear Christ, just a few days before his death, avow his mission to let the world know that to do God's will is, for him, to express his own will to love. Because for Christ, to accomplish the will of Him who has sent him is nothing but an alignment of his own will with his Father's will. The Father's will is a desire of love. To do the Father's will is to perform an act of love. Thus, when Christ prays: "Father, not my will, but yours!," he is asking that this desire to love should manifest the unity of love. We must not confuse this will to love with the will of someone wielding power. A filial relationship based on the son's fear of the dominating father would be unviable.

The unity of the father and the son is woven by reciprocity, by a perfect sharing: "All I have is yours and all you have is mine" (John 17:10). The Son's relationship to the Father is not one of subordination, of an inferior to a superior. It is an interdependence, in which each party recognizes the other as himself, loves the other as himself: "The Son can do nothing by himself; he can do only what he sees the Father doing: and whatever the Father does the Son does too. For the Father loves the Son and shows him every thing he does himself" (John 5:19-20). Thus, there is no conflict of personality between the Father and the Son. And thus, one may quite rigorously say, "Like Father, like Son." But also, "Like Son, like Father." For both of them reveal themselves to themselves *through one another*. A filial relationship that is not imbued with this gladdening joy of knowing that one is enriched by the other is not viable.

Christ reveals the Father to us by the manner in which he speaks of himself in terms of the Father. Jesus can tell his apostles, "I do not call you servants, but friends, for the servant does not know what the master does"; Jesus, in his relationship with the Father, has experienced the trust shown him by the Father. The Father shows the Son everything he does himself. And Christ also tells the disciples, "You will do greater things than I," because he recognizes that his Father is greater than he. "My Father is greater than I," he says. This does not mean that the Father is "above" the Son. Not at all. The Son simply recognizes that the Father is the prime source of Love, because it is the Father who sends Love. When the Father sends his Son on his earthly mission, He is responsible for the Son and the Son must reply to the Father with his faithfulness. A filial relationship denying the love relationship that creates its own special authority would also be unviable.

This attitude of "recognition" is the ideal of the filial relationship. In Jesus, it is expressed through worship. "Father, I glorify you." Adoration is the most radical expression of faith. The man who does not *adore* has not yet recognized God. The filial attitude is also expressed by one's joy of being oneself. Jesus would not be Jesus if he were not fully the

Son. He couldn't speak about the joy he promises us, if he did not recognize himself fully as the Son. He is speaking from experience.

His filial being is expressed by effacement. The Gospel never stops emphasizing this. Christ shows through in the Father's presence because he effaces himself before him. Effacing oneself does not mean disappearing, it means appearing in the light of him who allows you to be. "The Son can do nothing by himself" (John 5:19). That is why Christ prays to his Father: "Father, glorify me with that glory" (John 17:2 and 5). Jesus' entire filial being blossoms in his freedom to realize himself through the Other for the Other. This ecstasy (from the Greek roots meaning *being outside oneself*), this going out of oneself to find oneself again in the Other's heart, is also the essence of the Father's being.

The Father fulfills himself in him for whom he lives: his only Begotten Son, the "radiance of his Glory and the image of his substance." He who loses his life will find it," says Jesus. He knows what he's talking about. Not only because he himself has made the mystery of salvation come true with the gift of his life, but even more basically, because in his experience as the only Begotten Son, he knows that the Father is fully within his (Jesus') gift of himself to the world. That is what the Father manifests when Jesus is baptized in the Jordan; it is the only time that God's voice is heard: "This is my Son: I have placed all my love in him." Jesus is he to whom God can say: "My Love."

A filial relationship that is not imbued with such devotion and receptivity is unviable. The intrinsic characteristic of the filial relationship is to establish between the Father and the Son that admirable exchange in which He who gives himself is received in a giving love that gives itself again. The filial relationship is at the heart of all action of grace.

In the Name of the Son

For the Father, Jesus is everything. Jesus is his love. His desire to live, his will, his life, his being, his joy, his kingdom, his glory, his name. That's why Christ can tell the disciples, "What you will ask of the Father, he can give you in my name." Let us hasten to point out that Christ is not guaranteeing a fulfillment of prayers, as though the office of the Eternal Father had an automatic divine response for every request.

Jesus assures us that just as God cannot refuse his Beloved Son, so, too, he cannot refuse anything to man, whom he loves. However, man must not only ask as the Son would ask; he must ask in the name of the Son!

The Lord's Prayer, "Our Father," is Jesus' most perfect prayer. This prayer gives us his being. His reason to live. His happiness. It recapitulates the essence of what God asks us to believe. It makes us ask for the essential. Only great things: the Kingdom and the Bread. Love every day. And not to separate heaven and earth. In teaching the "unique prayer," Jesus invents nothing. He partly repeats the Kaddish—sanctification of the name—an ancient Aramaic prayer ending the service in synagogue. This text strongly emphasizes the Kingdom, the Glory, the Power of God. In his childhood Jesus blundered his way through this ancient prayer with other children his age, just as Christian children learn a definition in catechism word by word. And then he learned how to live it. He gave it a new meaning, a fullness it hadn't had before: and it is the filial meaning that he reveals to us. He tells us of the Kingdom that he proclaims by way of exploring the new meaning of forgiveness and deliverance from evil. Just as the great celebration of Passover became the Last Supper of the Lord, so, too, the Kaddish has found its full scope in the Lord's Prayer.

The early Church, still filled with the Judeo-Christian tradition and background of the apostles, did not forget the origins of the Lord's Prayer in the Kaddish. Thus, at the end of the Lord's Prayer, it added the doxology that was restored to Roman Catholic usage by Vatican Council II: "Yours is the Kingdom, the Power and the Glory forever and ever!" This acclamation, also found in Revelation, is quoted in the *Didache*, the teaching of the twelve apostles. Dating from the second century A.D., it is one of the oldest extant documents of the life of the earliest Christian communities.

The doxology has always been used in the Anglican Church and in most Protestant churches. By restoring this acclamation, the Roman Catholic Church was not only attempting a gesture of ecumenical rapproachment, it was also trying to go back to the roots of its purest tradition. Some people will most likely feel that, venerable as these words may be—*Kingdom, Power* and *Glory*—they no longer represent for today's Christians the rich treasure of tradition, which we have just cited. This, once again, is the difficult question of the language of faith: Should we omit these triumphal words on the pretext that they are no longer eloquent, but merely annoying; or should we invite Christians to rediscover the content of faith through traditional and sometimes archaic words?

As long as we are forced to find ways of speech suitable to prayer, the effort to find exactly the right word could well prevent us from praying, simply because we might never feel we *had* found the right words. We might never know how to pray. Which is precisely why Jesus taught us the Lord's Prayer, the one prayer we can all use with the minimum of debate.

Daring to Say . . .

In the end, it's essentially Jesus' filial stance that reveals to us who the Father is. One can discover the Father only by internalizing "the feelings that were those of the Christ Jesus." Why not, for instance, contemplate what Saint John informs us about Jesus' filial experience? His entire Gospel (especially the last parts of chapters five and seven, as well as chapter fourteen) are a veritable *summa* about the Father.

But meditation on the Father is fruitless if one does not purify one's heart of all the aggression created by bad images of the Father. A good number of Christians are quite indifferent to the wonder of being able, as baptized persons, to call God "Our Father." They find there is something excessive in it. Why does the liturgy make us repeat at each mass: "We *make bold* to say: 'Our Father!'"

Boldly, because nobody but the Only Begotten Son has the right to say "Father." Jesus gives us far more than the "right" to call his father "Our Father." He gives himself to us, so that, through him, we may be children of God and, in all truth, be virtually naturalized in God and put in touch with the divine. By being able to say "Our Father," we know that we are of God's stock and posterity. We know that we do not come from—nowhere. We know that we exist at least for someone. And infinitely so. We know that human fatherhood is wonderful, whatever its natural limits, for it is redeemed by God's fatherhood. We know that human fatherhood is possible because God's fatherhood is real. It reveals to us the potential riches of human fatherhood. And if the solitude of days without other people enters our lives, we know, at least, that there is no such thing as metaphysical solitude. God is a Father. He tells each one of us what Adonai said to his people through his prophet Isaiah:

> You are prized by me.
> You count in my eyes
> And I love you.

7

Jesus: Someone Spiritual.
God Is the Spirit.

Faith Is a Fire

Still, I must tell you the truth: it is for your own good that I am going; because unless I go, the Advocate will not come to you; but if I go, I will send him to you. And when he comes, he will show the world how wrong it was, about sin, and about who was in the right, and about judgment.... But when the Spirit of truth comes he will lead you to the complete truth, since he will not be speaking as from himself but will say only what he has learned; and he will tell you of the things to come. (John 16:7–8; 12–13)

Where Is He, Where Is He Not?

God. A pure spirit. The Father? He too is a spirit. And the Son? He too is a spirit. One might forget that the Father is a spirit. As for Christ, one forgets it all the more readily because Jesus became flesh. One forgets that Jesus' personality is in full possession of the Spirit. Not only the Holy Spirit is spirit. The Holy Spirit comes from the Father and the Son. He is no more mysterious than they. Merely less well-known. Misunderstood. The poor relative. The final, the third person—quite singular!

The Spirit is a living person. One cannot, obviously, say a person "of flesh and blood." And yet the reality of the Holy Spirit is as *true* as Christ's reality, but it eludes us even more than Christ's. The Spirit is felt, but ineffable. Where is the Spirit, where is he not? He is in God. He dwells in our hearts. He is at work in the world. He animates the church.

· **The Faces of the Spirit**
Opening Credits

Like the vast stage of a huge theater before a performance, the world is a huge, untilled emptiness. An immeasurably long black hole. At the first words of Genesis, the spotlights come up with dazzling brightness. They shine upon the Spirit.

"In the beginning, God created the heavens and the earth. Now the earth was a formless void, there was darkness over the deep, and God's spirit hovered over the waters" (Genesis 1:1-2). In these opening credits of Genesis, only one single name comes up: the Spirit. The scenery emerging half-seen from the shadows throw his silhouette into relief.

Heaven and earth—utter *tohu-bohu* (the Hebrew word for chaos). The spirit is there. In this deserted terrain. He acts as a stage director. One senses that the Spirit is the one who "reclaims the land."

Darkness covers the gaping mouth of this world that does not yet know itself. The Spirit turns on the light. He goes deep. He plumbs. He discerns.

The waters are primordial. Above them, hovers the Spirit. Amusingly enough, the French word *planer*, "to hover," also means "to be absent." But God wants to tell us the opposite. He expresses it by means of the image in Deuteronomy (32:11):

> Like an eagle watching its nest,
> hovering over its young,
> he spreads out his wings to hold him,
> he supports him on his pinions.

The Spirit is astonishingly present. An impregnating presence. A spellbinding presence. An indefectible presence. Have you ever tried to steal up to a bird? It flies away. Have you ever crept up to its nest? It remains. Anxiously peering, this sentinel will watch over its young, no matter what. The Spirit, taking under its wing that big nest—the world as yet unwarmed by fire—is the hot presence of motherly tenderness. God's opening credits are not yet given in their entirety. Still, we know enough to guess that the Spirit is the creativity of the Father, the fruitfulness that will make the Word flesh. But under what guises does it appear?

It Has an Air of the Wind

Spirit: *ruach* in Hebrew, *pneuma* in Greek; *spiritus* in Latin. These three tongues of the Revelation name the spirit with a word designating it as a puff of air. One is never outside the air. One is inside it. Air is made up of exchanges. It makes exchanges. In this divine environment—the Trinity and the world of human beings created in his image—the Spirit is a vital exchange. He is the biosphere of God and man. We are nourished by the Spirit as by the atmosphere, without which we could not live. Thus, all men share a common air: the air of God. But we do not all breathe at the same rate. The Spirit is the creator of all possible spaces. Thus, all sorts of men and women, black and white and yellow, and all the marvelously tanned skins, all the reddening colors, the thousand deepnesses of black, the thousand intensities of white, all the men who are marvelously male, all the women who are marvelously female, and all the children who are adorably childlike, aspire to this great air of God's.

Then, the wind comes up. The raging wind that can up-root the racist insanities among us. The wind of unity that, in its own way, displaces the petty freedoms we steal, the privileges that we take over, the rights that we give to our-selves. The wind gives each of us a clear field. As recalled by the delightful account of Jacob's meeting with Esau (Genesis 32 and 33), Esau was taken in by that scoundrel Jacob, who stole his birthright. The two brothers are dead-ly enemies, but now they are reconciled thanks to the Spirit. You need a change of air, it suggests to them. Each brother goes his own way, having, the Bible tells us, "a clear field." It is in the clear field that the wind rushes wildly, the wind that blends so powerfully with our earth that *clear field* and *wind* become a single word in a single name: the Spirit.

I will never tire of repeating what Saint John (3:8) quotes Jesus as saying: "Do not be surprised when I say. . . . The wind blows wherever it pleases; you hear its sound, but you cannot tell where it comes from or where it is going." The same is true of what is born of the Spirit. But how can this be? For it never foresees the wind. Indeed, one can't ever foresee it. Naturally, the weatherman makes his predic-tions; but who can blame specialists for being wrong about imponderables? The wind rises. How can we explain it? You will say that there are high-pressure and low-pressure systems. To which I rejoin: Why the particular low-pres-sure system we have today, rather than another? Meteorol-ogists explain the wind as a concatenation of phenomena; but why *this* concatenation? Where does the wind come from? One may have to be born in the wind, perhaps, to find out.

No one can stop the wind. No one can resist the tempest. People depend on the wind. The sailor knows this quite well when he is at the end of his rope. He steers, the boat surges into the wind, it heaves to. It takes you where you don't want to go. It took Saint Peter to Rome—and Christopher Columbus to America. The discovery of the New World was the surprise of the wind. The discovery of a new world is always a stroke of the Spirit.

The Devouring Fire

"I have come to bring fire to the earth, just as I would like it to be already lit!" Christ thereby announces the coming of the Spirit. Unlike the wind to which one gives one's body (have you ever leaned against the wind?), unlike water into which one dives, one does not *touch* fire. One gazes into it and succumbs to its fascination. But one keeps one's distance. One contemplates the Spirit, and the Spirit that lives in our hearts has a different dwelling with the Father and the Son. The Spirit is the transcendental, the completely other.

—Fire illuminates. Its brightness is not like that of the sun in broad daylight. Its light is circumscribed: it is heat in the depths of the night. The Spirit illuminates us; we have to be in the radiance of its focus.

—Fire warms so long as the embers are alive. The Spirit comforts so long as true enthusiasm rises from the ashes of illusion.

—Fire purifies. It transforms matter. The Spirit tests, it "shows the world how wrong it was, about sin, about who was in the right, and about judgment." It converts.

—Fire catches so long as you light it. The Spirit blazes so long as you seize the spark.

—Fire creates an atmosphere: gathered joy and shared silence. It is life. The Spirit creates the climate of God:

faith is the devouring fire of the Spirit, which burns throughout a lifetime.

Water and the Dove
God also says:

> "I will give you a new heart,
> I will put my spirit in you,
> I will pour a pure water upon you."
> (Ezekiel)

The heart is life. No heart, no life. The Spirit is the heart of God. The Spirit lives in our hearts in order to attune us to God's heartbeat. The human mind cannot *understand* the mysteries of God. The human heart *can* love God in his mystery. However, our hearts can be made of stone. The new heart is the Spirit in our hearts, capable of loving as God loves us.

Water is life. No water, no life. The Spirit is God bearing fruit. God in his best season! Water is fruitfulness, but it can also be a source of death: flood waters. That is why God speaks of pure water, the Living Water. This filtered water is the Spirit discerned, long-term fertility. And on the water—the bird! The water of Genesis, the water of the deluge, the water of baptism. In rain or shine or wind, the bird is at ease, it lives in the wind. And high, high up, it still flies. The bird is at home everywhere, and yet it prefers gardens. In the garden that it chooses, the bird sings when it feels like it. And the man or woman who listens is happy to know that an invisible bird is singing in the garden because it's morning and it feels like singing. The Spirit, God's feeling for human beings is there, always there, like the bird, invisible in its uncapturable freedom. This freedom so bewitched Saint John that he lists it as one of the most important characteristics of the Spirit. He calls the Spirit, "the Spirit of truth." The truth that sets us free!

• Who Is He, Who Is He Not?
The Spirit Is the Spirit

The air. The wind. The fire. The water. Decked out with all these elements of life, the Spirit should not be confused with some great God of nature. As the breath of life, it is indeed a Force of nature. Nevertheless, Christianity is not pantheistic. *"Spiritus domini replevit orbem terrarum...."* At Pentecost, we sing: "The Spirit of God has filled the universe." This fullness is not diluted in the world. The Spirit of God is a unique and distinct person, animating the entire cosmos, but not becoming part of it. The world has its own separate existence, and humans have their temporal life on earth. The intrinsic feature of the Spirit is that he penetrates to the heart of these autonomies, he respects each autonomy and enriches it with his presence. And since the center of the world, according to a lovely statement by André Turk, is the heart of man, this is the Holy of Holies of the Holy Spirit. How can one penetrate this innermost temple of God? Our experience with earthly fathers directs us towards the discovery of the Heavenly Father. However—as we have already said—it is essentially the revelation of Jesus that opens the mystery of the Father. The same applies to the Spirit. The "spiritual" experience of any spiritual person is an avenue by which that person may approach the Holy Spirit. But is is only the Revelation that allows us to know the Holy Spirit at all. Bear in mind: for all the continuity between the experience of human paternity and that of divine paternity, there is, above all and ultimately, discontinuity. A radical difference. Likewise, between the human spritual experience and the experience of the Spirit in faith, there is a continuity, but also a difference. However, in the domain of the Spirit, this difference does not appear so vast because it is less distinct. There is a vast and apparent abyss between the poverty of earthly fathers and the riches of the Heavenly Father. We less easily see the gap between an authentic human spiritual experience and the discovery of the Spirit as a being "who dwells in our hearts," for this discovery is possible only within human spiritual experience. Thus, we always run a risk of diminishing the Spirit to *spirit*.

The Joining

In the New Testament, especially in Saint Paul, it is sometimes hard to tell whether the word *Spirit* designates the Holy Spirit or man's spirit. This telescoping indicates the close communion between God's Spirit and man's spirit. Saint Paul says (Romans 8:16): "The Spirit of God joins our spirit with him." How can we find the link? We do not want to draw an absolute demarcation line between the domain of man's spirit and the domain of God's Spirit; but we should try not to confuse the two domains. One can be spiritual without being Christian—that is, one can recognize a finality of existence in the spiritual values of life. Christian faith is not pure spirituality. It is not content with assigning priority to the spiritual values of life. It is spiritual life in that it makes the Christian "a spiritual man" (I Corinthians 3) in quest of God the Spirit. Saint Paul speaks of the relationship "with the Christ in the Spirit" or "in the Christ with the Spirit." These two formulas are interchangeable. The Scripture doesn't seem to address the subtlety of the correlation of the Father, the Son, and the Spirit with one another and with us.

Scripture emphasizes the full sway that the life of the Spirit has upon the life of every person. Sometimes, he pounces lightning-swift upon man, like the eagle swooping down upon the lamb: recall Samson (Judges 14:6): "The spirit of God seized on him, and though he had no weapon in his hand he tore the lion in pieces as a man tears a kid." Sometimes, as gentle as a silent tide licking its way up a beach, he calmly reaches out to man: thus, the Spirit "rests upon Isaiah," "covers Mary with his shadow," "hovers over Jesus in the Jordan." These images tell us that however he may act, the Spirit takes the entire person. Saint Paul expressed this hold according to the Greek view of humans in his time. The Greek language has two words for *spirit*. This makes things easier, for then we know what we're talking about. *Pneuma* is the Spirit of God and *nous* is the spirit of man. Attempting to express the unity of this Spirit of God, which joins the spirit of man, Saint Paul, in the First Letter to the Thessalonians, a basic text to the understanding of the relationship sees the situation on four levels (5:23)

—the Spirit of God, *pneuma*, the breath of life;
—the spirit of man, *nous*, the intellectual faculties;
—*psyche*, man's sensibilities;
—and finally, *soma*, the body.

Flesh Body, Spiritual Body

It's very important to integrate the body into this full vision of man! This unity should be stressed all the more since Saint Paul puts the flesh in stark opposition to the spirit, pitilessly railing against the works of the flesh, the works of death. Indeed, when Saint Paul speaks of the works of the flesh, he doesn't always mean "flesh" in the Hebrew sense. For Semites, the flesh is the entire being. This was what Isaiah meant when he said: "All flesh will see salvation." For Saint Paul, flesh most often refers exclusively to the carnal aspects of humans. Like Saint John, who says "What is born of the flesh is flesh, what is of the Spirit is Spirit," Saint Paul affirms in the Letter to the Romans (8:5–9): "Those who live by the flesh desire what is carnal, those who live by the Spirit desire what is spiritual. For the desire of the flesh (carnal) is death, while the desire for the Spirit is life and peace, because the desire of the flesh is the enemy of God. You are not in the flesh, but in the Spirit, because the Spirit of God lives within you."

The body is flesh, but not *only* carnal. In this way, if one places flesh and spirit in opposition, one cannot oppose them as if the spirit could live without the body and the body without the spirit. To admit this body-spirit dualism would undercut the reality of Jesus Christ Incarnate. It would deny the unity of the person that the Risen Christ manifests in his "spiritual body." True, our bodies are not yet fully spiritual; but if we agree with Paul's affirmation that "we are already resurrected," then we must be able to say, "Our bodies are already spiritual in strength."

At the moment, Hinduism is attracting many Christians. This attraction is not unambiguous. Granted, it expresses an authentic desire for inner disencumberment, the rejection of a material world that judges the worth of people by the horsepower of their cars. Challenging the grossness of a pot-bellied world sometimes takes the form of escape, withdrawal. It may be easier to break away on the heights of a pantheism in which the spirit is diluted than to commit oneself to living the Beatitudes and the "Our Father" that incarnate the Spirit. The Spirit of God is not outside life. It is the Light of life. It is life operating in the darkness of each day: "Because the Spirit is our life, because the Spirit also makes us act!" The Christian's spiritual life *is* made flesh. If someone claims to be seeking the Spirit while avoiding the world and his brethren, he or she may be a good person but is not truly caught up in the Spirit.

• The Face of the Spirit
The Common Noun

Scripture tells us less about who the Spirit is than what he does. And for good reason! He is action. Action that transforms. With the Spirit, "things change!" With the Spirit one can hope to see the world improve. The Spirit changes the course of history just as it changes our inmost hearts. This action is manifested throughout the history of the people of God. The face of the Spirit is confused with the features of its dynamism. This dynamism is expressed— very nearly—according to a pattern that recurs in various circumstances: God's Word calls the people together (for instance, Moses on Mount Sinai). God makes a covenant. He leads his people by working wonders (for instance, the manna falling in the desert). The people evolves, passes from state to state, converts little by little (the crossing of the Red Sea, the crossing of the Jordan, the Exile, the Return). The Old Testament does not yet reveal the Spirit as a person. However, it suggests the person by letting the presence of the Spirit emerge on the surface of events. This presence is manifested as a force coming not from man but from elsewhere, a transcendant force, the holiness of God, who ultimately overcomes sin. Thus, David, after murdering Uriah, realizes that he is "that man" capable of that sordid crime. The Spirit creates a new heart within him. A pure heart.

We must await the New Testament to learn that God is not alone, Jesus reveals the Father to us. He reveals him in the Spirit. One could apply to the Spirit the words that Jesus speaks to Philip about the Father: "He who sees me sees the Father," he who sees me sees the Spirit. Indeed, just as everything that Christ does expresses something of the action of the Spirit. The Spirit is all One and all the Other: the Father and the Son. It's no use figuring out whom he resembles more. Certain appellations make him look more like the Father: Jesus says "Holy Father." And he calls the Spirit the "Holy Spirit." Sometimes, Jesus compares himself to the Spirit. Jesus calls himself the Truth, while he quite naturally likes to call the Spirit what he calls himself: the Spirit of Truth. But the trait that most aptly characterizes the Spirit seems to be holiness.

The evangelists, marked by the catechetic concern of the early communities, stress the fact that the Spirit is the *Holy*

Spirit. They want to make it clear that the Spirit is someone. He who sanctifies is he who can perfectly communicate the Love of the Father and of the Son. He who purifies. He who "proves the world wrong about sin."

In the three synoptic Gospels, Jesus does not seem to apply the word *Holy* all that much to the Spirit. He normally calls him "Spirit" pure and simple, or the "Spirit of God." Saint John has Jesus say that the Spirit is the Advocate, the Paraclete.

The Proper Noun
Paraclete is a curious Greek word. It cannot be translated literally. It has the advantage of being a name, a proper noun. It has no equivalent in French or English. It refers to "an advocate or lawyer who does not drop his client." It is customarily translated into French as *Consolateur* (Consoler, Comforter). Christ, it seems, wishes to assure us of an unflagging presence. A presence of love, a presence of him who takes up the defense and pleads the case, identifying the truth.

The Spirit of Truth: If we are to believe Saint John, this seems to be Christ's preferred appellation for the Spirit. Which comes as no surprise. Holiness and Truth go hand in hand. Truth affects being. Being true means being oneself. The Spirit makes the truth. He makes sure that he is himself. He makes sure that we are ourselves. But in order to become ourselves, we must—as has been repeated several times—become *otherwise*. Because the Spirit of Truth is the Holy Spirit, we know that this truth he creates in us is not only a supreme value, it is the communication of his very being. Through the Holy Spirit, we are brought into the communion of the Father and the Son. As a source of holiness, he lets us take part in the glory that he has communicated to Christ by resurrecting him. This is the truth of the Spirit.

The Spirit of Promise (Ephesians 1:13)

It is the Resurrection that manifests the holiness of the Spirit. I don't know whether you've noticed this explosive verse (John 7:39): "There was no Spirit as yet because Jesus has not yet been glorified." The Spirit has not yet been "known," because he had not yet been recognized as he who could work any transformation. In God himself, the supreme gift of the Spirit is, above all, this communication of the power of resurrection, the true source of holiness.

Just as the Word was not the Word Made Flesh before the birth of Jesus, so too, the Spirit was not yet the Spirit of Christ Risen before Pentecost, an ultimate realization of the Easter mystery. The Spirit is put into the world in the very act that gives birth to the church. Hence, it appears that the Spirit does not give his strength as though he came from outside. The gifts of the Spirit are *not* ways of living as a Christian; they are the very life of Christ resurrected in us.

For the Spirit, sanctifying does not mean giving man the means to become holy; it means being one with him, creating him, recreating him. For the Spirit, sanctifying means remaining as the Holy in the warmth of our lives as sinners and, hence, revealing to us that we are apart and different from our sinning. Of the three synoptics, Saint Luke is probably the one most sensitive to this presence of the Spirit "filling" the heart of man, filling the church at the heart of the world. The word *fill* is a quantitative image; but it evokes the quality of the Spirit going to the extreme of what it is, of what it does. Thus, at the birth of Saint John the Baptist and at the birth of Jesus, Saint Luke shows us that the Spirit has done the impossible. The Spirit operates as only God can operate. The Acts of the Apostles—which has been called the book of the Spirit—exalts the marvels and wonders that are uniquely worked not only for individuals, but for entire communities. It is the Spirit, for instance, who makes this emerging church of the Pentecost grow. The Spririt then deploys its gifts and charismas.

• The Achievements of the Spirit:
Freedom, Unity, Inequality

The gifts of the Spirit should obviously not be limited to the traditional septenary, that is, the "classical" seven gifts that nourished popular piety for centuries and that simply bear the features of Emmanuel as depicted by Isaiah (Chapter 7). On the one hand, the liberality of these exceptional gifts emphasizes the inexhaustible freedom of him who acts as he likes "at all times and in all fashion." On the other hand, this prodigality reminds us that Christian unity is the opposite of uniformity, because, in essence, it is the unity of God in three different persons.

Saint Paul, in his letters, often returns to the theme of unity, a theme with immediate impact on the life of com-munities. It is always a topical theme. In the church, the many gifts and charismas of the Spirit help create a spirit of healthy competition and exchange between individuals and a rich variety of options and paths of action. Since it is the same Spirit acting on both sides of any given debate or exchange, it makes it possible to believe that Unity is possible. But the action of the Holy Spirit does not lead to the leveling-off of human potential. The Spirit forms a unity with men who are equal in nature, but differing and unequal in intelligence, spirit, heart, and potential. The Holy Spirit does not promote a bland atmosphere of "sweetness and light." Whether on the level of relations among Roman Catholics, ecumenical relations among Christians, or relations with non-believers, this unity is built in the thick of con-frontations, disputes. It's been said a thousand times and perhaps should be said once again: unity is not the absence of conflict. What we have to watch is the very *human* Christian knack for watering things down in the name of equality and charity. But that is *not* what the Holy Spirit is about.

The Meaning of the Spirit

In the face of a given disagreement in need of resolution, how can we be sure of achieving unity? If a certain action must be carried out, a certain decision reached, how can we tell whether our choice of action or the decision arrived at has been inspired by the Spirit of truth? Discerning the Spirit is not an emotional matter. One can only discern the meaning of the Spirit's action in its own realm, in the place where it moves: the realm of truth, freedom, unity.

Any seeker after the truth must start by placing himself or herself in a position to receive the truth. One acquires the sense of the Spirit by participating in the life of the Spirit. But this perception is not infallible. We are told we shouldn't worry about how to respond to our persecutors, because, Jesus says, "it is not you who will be speaking; the Spirit . . . will be speaking in you" (Matthew 10:20). We are promised the Spirit, but we are not promised that we will never make a mistake.

Where the Spirit Is

Only the Spirit is infallible. When Roman Catholics call the Pope infallible, they simply mean that the Spirit acting in him cannot be in error or deal wrongly with them to the extent that the Pope is fully inspired "in matters of faith." For "where the Church is, that is where the Spirit is." However, the church is more than the Pope. It is more than each of us, than each of our communities. It is more than itself because it is called upon by its internal dynamism to keep growing endlessly in order to become the whole, complete Body of Christ. It is in the ever-expanding terms of God's infinity that the church is the measure of the Spirit. It is in the church that one discerns the Spirit, for the Spirit knows the inner life of the church more totally than the church knows its own life.

In practical terms, it is actually the confrontation of diverse points of view that gives us the hope of making these words of Christ's come true: "Wherever two or three are united in my name, I am there with them." I say *hope*, for one cannot use Christ's words to claim a monopoly of the Spirit on the pretext of being united in his name. Who can claim to be purely united in Christ's name? When the church says it is united in Christ's name, then, whether conciliar or synodical, parochial or otherwise, isn't the church also apt to be united on behalf of divergent interests within the body seeking to defend, their own positions and gain acceptance for them against opposing ideas. Isn't the church sometimes united out of fear and to meet various internal and external crises? So let's not go too fast.

"Wherever the church is, the Spirit may not always be," for the church, as the source of holiness, is a gathering of sinners. Likewise, with all due respect to Saint Irenaeus, who is quoted without rhyme or reason: "Where the Spirit is, the church may not always be *necessarily*."

If the Spirit renews the faith in the world, I would say: "Wherever the Spirit is, there is the world," the world of human beings called upon to become the Kingdom of God. If the "spirit of the world" is a hindrance to this growth then perhaps it's because the church, too, has its "church spirit," its ecclesiastical, institutional spirit, its "Sistine Chapel" spirit, which often prevents the world from understanding and attaining faith as God's devouring fire that would consume the world.

But Roman Catholics shouldn't just look accusingly at Rome as the source of their problems of faith. If I mention the Sistine Chapel, this doesn't mean that we should forget the myriad problems in our own home parishes and blame the Vatican for everything. Like the Sistine Chapel, parish churches also have decorated ceilings which hide the beauty of the sky. All of us have our triumphalist moments.

It is only in that transparency of faith known as humility,

in a breath of pure air, that the Spirit can live and be discerned. The Christ who said, "My Father is greater than I," also said in his awareness of the Spirit, "I must leave," "I must efface myself." Today's church, coping with a world that yearns for the Spirit, need not do anything, perhaps, but try to fulfill these words of Saint John the Baptist: "He must grow greater, I must grow smaller" (John 3:30).

> It is good, Lord,
> to thank you
> for the gift of your Spirit
> the Promise kept by Jesus Christ!
>
> Spirit of God
> it's not trivial to call you
> by your name: Spirit of Truth
> the name that Jesus gave you!
>
> Spirit of Truth, Spirit of Unity
> the same Spirit . . .
> breathe life in us, prompt us
> with human words
> We want to give you our Word
> A Word of Unity!
>
> Spirit of all joy
> Source of our faith
> You confirm your presence
> With the signs of Hope.
>
> We thank you.

> > For the taste of Unity
> > the revelation of your intimacy
> >
> > For this fire that burns in our hearts
> > the hope for a better world
> >
> > for so much love that may never be seen
> > and which through you may become
> > the Seed of Peace!

8

Jesus: Born of a Woman
Mary, Mother of God
Faith Is Life-Bearing

Now a great sign appeared in heaven: a woman adorned with the sun, standing on the moon, and with the twelve stars on her head for a crown: She was pregnant and in labor, crying aloud in the pangs of childbirth. Then a second sign appeared in the sky, a huge red dragon which had seven heads and ten horns, and each of the seven heads crowned with a coronet. Its tail dragged a third of the stars from the sky and dropped them to the earth, and the dragon stopped in front of the woman as she was having the child, so that he could eat it as soon as it was born from its mother. The woman brought a male child into the world, the son who was to rule all the nations with an iron scepter, and the child was taken straight up to God and to his throne.

(Revelation 12:1–5)

"A Great Sign . . . . A Woman!"

Jesus, the son of God, "born of a woman," according to Saint Paul's Letter to the Galatians (4:4), was brought into the world by a rare woman, whom some claim to see in this description in Revelations. An astonishing woman, Mary. Wondrous, yet never working any wonder. She, the "yes" of God, never said anything. She did not speak. She left no writings. No testament. But wait: she did leave a testament: Jesus Christ! Mary, Mother of God: This is the great, the true title of the Virgin. This one fact means everything. Christ: Mary's whole reason for existing.

Between her true importance and her ascribed importance lies the clutter of centuries of Christian belief. Mary has collapsed under the weight of titles and crowns. She is a mediator. A comforter. A co-redeemer. She is queen of everything: the universe, the clergy, the missions, the Holy Childhood. She is the patron of practically all Roman Catholic cathedrals, hundreds of religious congregations, thousands of works and projects. When you paint a Romanesque Virgin in gaudy colors, she turns, Baroque. Baroque art, made up of endless visual small talk, is ultimately a sign of decadence. By suffocating the Virgin in a devotion that "lays it on thick," we no longer see her real face. By using too many miraculous medals and objects of a patchwork piety, Christians have tried to make her the privileged means of approaching God. "To Jesus through Mary!" As though there weren't enough hindrances to finding God along the road of faith: the church, revelation, the sacraments, morality, priests, the Holy Virgin. What an obstacle course!

However, Mary *is* a presence on the road of faith. A presence is not a means. To say that Mary is the best means for "going to Jesus" gives the wrong impression to people who are strangers to the mystery of the Virgin. Doesn't it make it look as if you have to pull strings to approach God? I prefer the term *presence*, because it implies a free encounter. Mary does not impose her mediation. When someone invokes it with the words "Our Lady of Perpetual Help," what does he mean? Quite simply that Mary can be and do something for us. There is no gap between heaven and earth. Heaven is the state of communion in which beings can do or be something for other beings. If the Mother of God is among these beings, then, understandably, the Church's faith would be poorer if Christians did not give her the proper respect and, prime among the saints, ask her intercession. Popular faith does not err. There's nothing trivial in the words, repeated for centuries: "Holy Mary, mother of God, pray for us sinners now and in the hour of our death."

The effectiveness of Mary's presence is like a sacrament for us. I prefer to say "Virgin as sacrament" rather than "Virgin as means." To speak of the Virgin as a sacrament simply means: by token of her presence, Mary reveals the wonders of God to us. In the glory of the Resurrection, she is, invisibly, the witness to the New World. "Full of grace," she is perfectly beautiful: isn't beauty grace?

The Virgin's beauty interests us because beauty is gratuitous. What is belief if not a gratuitous act? Mary's beauty predisposes us to believe. Admiring Mary's beauty obviously doesn't mean that her eyes are more beautiful than ours. Mary's beauty wouldn't get her into a Miss Universe contest. Mary, "blessed among women," is beautiful because God placed all his loving kindness in her. But because Mary effaces herself (and her modesty is an important part of her beauty), she presents God to us; she reveals to us in all the events of her life—from her conception to her assumption —that the essential thing is God.

• The Essential Thing Is God
From Conception to Assumption

The Immaculate Conception is not a privilege that God granted Mary out of a kind of divine favoritism. Why was this historic exception made? Did Jesus Christ confer it so that he himself would escape the heritage of original sin? Naturally, Christ is without sin, and there is no possibility of doubting that Mary is exempt from original sin. One can, however, wonder about the meaning of this exemption. The Savior, we assume, could not be born of a creature marked by original sin. But didn't Jesus receive, in the Jordan, the baptism of repentance, which established his solidarity, his oneness with sinners? Couldn't Jesus, without being a sinner himself, have been born in solidarity with all humans—who are born sinners? This original solidarity with human beings does not seem to have prevented Christ from manifesting his inalterable holiness and his power to liberate humans from sin; for it is essentially by his Resurrection that Christ manifested the power of salvation, and not by his exemption from original sin.

The Immaculate Conception is possible because of God's sovereign freedom in his creation. All human beings are born sinners. However, if God wishes, he can let a woman be born without sin. This exemption from sin reveals to us that the heredity of sin shouldn't be viewed as an absolute determinism of evil: it shows us at least one woman who has lost nothing of her beauty and has wasted none of her talents. Through Mary Immaculate, we know that faithfulness is possible. Mary manifests the glory of God's vision of mankind as it might have been—not a paradisal myth but as a real person. Unfortunately, the term *Immaculate* bristles with ambiguities. It evokes purity; and for generations, purity has been confined to the sexual realm. The purity implied by the Immaculate Conception is nothing but the transparency, the perfect responsiveness to God's will.

Such faithfulness does not exclude Mary from the mystery of salvation. The Magnificat bears witness to this, be-

cause it is a paean of praise to the wonders of salvation that
Mary experiences in herself. Mary makes us realize that salvation is not merely the forgivensss of sins, but also the communication of God's bounty to the lives and hearts of a redeemed humanity. Even if Adam hadn't sinned, he would
nevertheless have had to receive the mystery of salvation.
At their best and most viruous, a man or woman must be
enriched by God. The fact that we are naturally capable of
beauty, of goodness is one of the positive signs of salvation.
Salvation should not be viewed merely as the reparation of
the worst, but also as the creation of the best. This positive
character of salvation was manifested in the assumption of
the Virgin.

Mary's assumption, first of all, proves the success of her
life. Throughout her life, Mary was able to assume what
she had to live in light of the resurrection to come. The
word *assumption* comes from the verb *assume*. To believe
in Mary's assumption is to believe that the Virgin, who lived
like us, is resurrected today. Mary's assumption is not just
the final crowning of the queen. It is the sign of the success
of our destiny. The Risen Christ lifts us up with the power
of his own Resurrection. Because at least one woman, a human woman, is invested with this success, we can have the
hope of what we do not see. We can speak of the Assumption in terms of a visitation. Just as Mary went to visit her
cousin Elizabeth to share God's joy in her, so too, the Virgin, by communicating this hope to us, continues to "visit
the earth," because she is the sign of the Resurrection for the
entire world.

From the immaculate conception to the glory of the
assumption, Mary is the sign to people of their own destiny. She knows what she's talking about. She announces to
human beings that which was announced to her. She announces to them that there is more than one annunciation
in life.

The Annunciations

"The angel of the Lord announced to Mary that she would be the mother of the Savior." We can always wonder whether this announcement was perceived by the Virgin through an inner vision or if it came through an actual intervention by God making himself known through an angel. No matter. The Virgin, it seems, must have glimpsed the enormity, the totality of the mystery that opened up to her. And she said yes. It's pointless asking whether Mary could have refused to become the mother of God. Would God then have had to look for another woman to be the mother of his Son? It seems plain that Mary could only answer yes because she was she and no one else. Being immaculate, she is in full possession of herself. And self-possessed freedom means consenting only to goodness. Mary reveals to us that human freedom is more than free choice. Freedom doesn't consist purely in choosing between good and evil; it also implies consenting to be what one is. Mary's faithfulness is the expression of that full freedom of going along with God's will. But how did she perceive God's will?

The enthusiasm of the Magnificat, her hymn of praise, leads us to think that Mary, first of all, sees that God believes in her. One cannot discover God's will if one doesn't believe he cares for us. God believes in Mary because he loves her for herself. He doesn't use her as a pawn to carry out his plans. Thus, in contrast to Zechariah, who doubts and then loses the power of speech at the announcement of the birth of John the Baptist, Mary is utterly delighted. She cries: "The Mighty One has worked wonders for me!" She can apply to herself the words of Ann's hymn in the Old Testament, for she verifies within herself what the Spirit manifests: "He raises the humble."

Mary is not the only one who can say: "God does great things in me!" Everyone is called upon to recognize God's workings in himself. One cannot believe in God and remain outside oneself. God is within us. One discovers God through everything that one is and that one is called upon to be, in other words, through "one's" calling. But admitting we have a calling is not a matter of course. The transparency, the attentive calm, of the Virgin is required for us to accept belief that God calls upon us, each of us, to carry out something of his plan. The manner in which the Virgin agrees "to have a calling" is, for us, a sign of faith. Mary doesn't argue. She displays "no false humility." She doesn't reply that she is not worthy, not able. Faith is beyond worthiness and even capability.

Filled with the audacity of faith, Mary, in the Magnificat, can thus sing in advance the beatitudes of her Son. "He raises the humble, he feeds the hungry." Where has the Virgin seen any of these things? She sees Herod quite in place: and he's the one who'll send her Son away! The streets are filled with the poor, and she knows it. People tread on the feet of the humble. And the rich have their own way of eyeing you. But because Mary has the vision of a justified world, because she has the "key to salvation," she can already understand her Son, who will eventually say to her: "Blessed are the poor."

Between the announcement of salvation, which came about thanks to her, and its full realization, Mary, like us, had to discover, on the very day, the coming of the Kingdom which is here and which is to come. Rather like baptism plunging us once and for all into death and resurrection, the "yes" of the annunciation plunged Mary into the mystery to which she had to consent to every day. The faith that commits one's entire being in a definitive way is inscribed in time and expressed in privileged moments. The believers need precise moments in which this fundamental commitment is marked. That's why Christian life has sacraments, rites, festivals, liturgy, which are just so many announcements of salvation. That's why a human life has decisions, options, which are just so many authentifications of the commitment of a whole life. The commitment of faith, that is, the commitment of the whole person in God is seen through many situations such as the Virgin lives through in the course of her life: she had to say "yes" again in Bethlehem, in Egypt, in Nazareth, in Cana, in Jerusalem, at Golgotha. If we were more attentive to the "news" that each event constitutes in our lives, we might more effectively perceive that there are as many annunciations in a life as there are situations to live through. The Christian's calling, too often spoken of as though it were a unique, lightning-swift event, is never isolated from the rest of his life. Thus, each human being, married or not, with a religious vocation or not, a priest or not, ceaselessly discovers his or her calling throughout life. Ten, twenty, thirty years after a fundamental choice, he discovers his true calling through other choices facing him. Man's calling is never behind him. It is always ahead of him.

· The Important Thing Is the Child
The Laughter of Faith

The Annunciation to Mary twenty centuries ago is an announcement made to all people in all times. The announcement of their calling to give birth to Jesus Christ in their lives. In her silence of two thousand years, the Virgin has only one thing to tell us: The important thing is the Child. In other words, Mary's virginity makes sense only because of her motherhood. There is no evangelical virginity without fruitfulness. Virginity is always commanded to the Other. Virginity and fruitfulness express the dynamism of all Christian life. Because Mary experienced both virginity and fruitfulness in her person, it becomes easier for us to understand more clearly that virginity and fruitfulness complement one another. There is no true fruitfulness without the humility implied by virginity. There is no blossoming virginity without the gift of self implied by all fruitfulness. To ask today about Mary's fruitful virginity is to ask about the meaning of fruitfulness in evangelical life.

We are far from being on the verge of comprehending the "how" of Mary's virginity. How could the mother of Jesus conceive her child without having had sexual relations with her husband? No doubt, from era to era, skeptical generations have smiled at this Virgin. A foolish virgin? One speaks of an action by the Holy Spirit. What action would scientists speak of? "The Holy Spirit will come upon you and the power of the Most High will take you under its shadow." An answer that can be received only in faith. This shadow is the equivalent of the cloud, a traditional element in the Old Testament theophanies, that is, manifestations of God. What is revealed to us in the Annunciation is classical: God intervenes, as he alone can intervene, with the sovereign power of his absolute freedom. But since God is not in the habit of short-circuiting natural phenomena, it is normal for science, within its own domain, to seek hypotheses allowing this divine intervention to dovetail with the known data of life. Thus, one speaks of parthenogenesis. I obviously can't venture onto this shaky ground, where I have no competence; all I can do is point out that, according to certain scientists, natural parthenogenesis can give birth only to girls. So we're back to the mystery. As with any mystery, it's as useless trying to explain it as it's cowardly to give up and not try to understand it. I'm reminded of what Pascal said: "Humiliate yourself, impotent reason!" However, I prefer his other *pensée*: "The ultimate measure of reason is to acknowledge that there is an infinity of things beyond it."

A mystery always invites us to see further than the mystery. A mystery is a night whose day is in the other hemisphere. God is not done with astonishing man. God, I think, must laugh his head off, seeing our brows furrow at some mystery that titillates us even more than others. If God is the Trinity, that's his business! It's easier to accept this than the things that are *our* business. Trying to cope with the fruitfulness of the Virgin, Saint Luke is at the end of his arguments: "For God, nothing is impossible!" This is implicitly what the author of Genesis says about Sarah: "Is anything too wondrous for God?" Sarah, an old, sterile woman could not believe in this improbable promise: How could she, a withered crone, bring a son into the world? At her age? What a laugh. And indeed she laughed. In Sarah's laughter, God himself burst into guffaws at having once more the most unexpected way to carry out his plans. An old woman was to give Abraham, father of the believers, the first son of the people of God. A girl who has never known a man was to give mankind the Only Begotten Son, "First-born of Creation." According to Saint Paul's language, this birth shows us that God likes what is weak in order to confound the wise. God did not wait for Erasmus to voice the praise of folly. Mary's virginity teaches us that God works wonders because he is a wondrous God. God does the impossible because he is an impossible God. But when God asks for the impossible, he always gives the impossible. He gives himself to the Virgin: "You are blessed among women! The Lord is with you...." Make us laugh even more, little Mary.... The laughter of faith has never been so necessary!

If the "how" of Mary's virginity remains unfathomable, the "why" may be more accessible. For a long time, there was one theological argument transcendent over other theological opinions. One may think what one likes: Jesus Christ, Son of God, "begotten but not made," could not receive his life from a finite creature. It is he, the eternal Word, who gives life to all being. How could a creature give life to him who is its origin? Mary is not at the origin of

God's life, she is its mediation. By remaining a virgin, Mary shows that Jesus comes only from the Father of the heavens and not "from a human will." One can accept this argument up to a point. However, it contains what we've said about the immaculate conception: it is essentially through the resurrection, and not through the origins of his human birth, that Christ manifests his freedom from the origin of life. But then why did Christ place himself outside the fleshly contingencies of human conception? Wouldn't it seriously impair the veracity of the incarnation to start by escaping that which constitutes the human condition?

People have actually gone so far as to think that it would have been unworthy of Christ to be the fruit of a sexual relation. But God became flesh. Flesh of our flesh. Why would he have been afraid of flesh? Mary's virginity is no trick that God thought up to escape sexual realities. So what can we say? At most, that the mystery of Mary's virginity denotes a certain humility in the presence of the power of life that God gives humans. By way of her fruitful virginity, Mary reminds us that, strictly speaking, human beings do not *give* life, they merely *transmit* it. Virginity asks us to receive all fruitfulness as coming from God. The extraordinary human power to give birth is even more extraordinarily dependent on the Creator. The Christian notion of fruitfulness involves seeing all life as a gift of God.

There are other reasons for the virginal conception of Christ. It instantly places his humanity in the dimension of eternity. In the Kingdom, the Gospel tells us, "there will be no male and no female." This does not mean that we will lose our identities. On the contrary, we will know one another as we are known. There will be no more secrecy for anyone. We will encounter one another with no ulterior motives. We will recognize one another in broad daylight. We will communicate universally, beyond the enclosure that sexual privacy inevitably creates. This perfect communication with the other in universal availability, this power to give the other something of one's own life—this is a token of the fruitfulness of this virginity, a true sign of the Kingdom.

Virgin and Mother

To understand the meaning of the fruitfulness of Christian virginity, one must, first of all, make sure that one does not see it in terms of pagan virginity. In ancient religions, virginity was sometimes used as a part of the consecration of a cult to sexual power. Paradoxically, sexual power was exalted by its opposite: the negation of sex. For men, this was translated into forced virginity—castration —and for women, cloistering. Thus, the priestesses of the goddess Vesta were, in practice, sacrificed to the sexual taboo, threatened with being buried alive if they broke their vow of celibacy.

Christian virginity does not express sexual taboos. In itself, sex is a good thing. In itself, a lack of sexual relations is senseless. Virginity is no end in itself. Its value lies purely in the extent to which it permits one to join the other *beyond* the limits of carnal dialogue. Sex creates a close communion with the other, so close as to inevitably reduce the sexual partners to an exclusive twosome. Virginity, in its desire to join the other univerally, beyond carnal relations, testifies to a will to love without bounds. This doesn't mean that married people are locked up as a couple, unable to communicate with others in great openness. We all know married people who are far more available than single people locked into relationships with others. We must simply bear in mind that virginity can be the sign of universal love only if it expresses the mystery of Christ's love, which is inseparable from the mystery of his death and resurrection. An aspect of death is seen in the inherent poverty and solitude of virginity. The aspect of resurrection is seen in the joy of creating life all around.

—Poverty. Yes; so long as one lives through what Christ lived through in his death and resurrection: "This is my body delivered . . . this is my body given . . . ," given universally and not returned. The gift of his body—body and soul—is a sign of the Kingdom. Agreeing not to give everything that the body—body and soul— could give, agreeing not to receive everything that the body—body and soul— could receive is a form of basic poverty, easily forgotten, that established the Christian in an unspectacular and yet profound solidarity with the poorest of the poor. It is a solidarity with all those who don't even have the power to transmit life. Solidarity with all those who do have the power to transmit life, but who, at loggerheads as a couple, can no longer experience the joy of this power. In this respect, it is obvious that virginity is not just the lot of the unmarried. All married people are destined to experience a certain form of virginity in marriage, if only in the poverty that they may discover within their marriage.

—Solitude. Yes; so long as one lives through the solitude of contemplation that Christ, dead and risen, lived through. An unromantic solitude. A solitude that does not imprison in isolation. A solitude that is all the more open to others in that it is a presence in itself. Positive solitude is the skill of accepting oneself for oneself, and others for others. One can welcome others only if one first welcomes oneself. This is the Virgin's testimony throughout her life, especially in the mystery of the Visitation. Remaining inside herself and at the same time coming out of herself, the Virgin goes toward Elizabeth to receive her joy and give her her own joy in return, making life grow in this sharing.

By means of everything that one is, to give something of the inner meaning of one's life, to pass on the breath of the

Spirit and, in many ways, to allow others to live, perhaps simply because of one's existence—such is the fruitfulness of virginity experienced as an expression of the resurrection of Christ. There is no happy virginity save the one that gives life. As the Virgin, Mary was the fruitful Mother, not only because she allowed Christ to see the light of day, but also because her existence as a woman was a vital presence for Christ.

Even today, when many men and women forgo starting a home and procreating, theirs is not a sterile act without consequences, it is a sign of the Absoluteness of God, who asks us to view our life beyond the relative limits of our existence. One cannot experience virginity without seeing the human life of one's time in terms of the end of time. An eschatological perspective, as the theologians would call it. Until the Second Coming of Christ, the acceptance of virginity informs the people of earth of the unique mission of virginity to bring into the world the Only Begotten Child: Jesus Christ. Even if the world refuses to recognize this appeal, it still must be made. However, we must acknowledge that virginity in our day is more difficult because the world is less willing to receive such testimony.

Virginity is an uncomfortable state of life; but this doesn't make it a feat that men and women, stronger than others, can perform on their own. For centuries, there was enough suspicion of both carnal realities and of the arrogance of virgins in the church to end the belief that virginity is a state of perfection reserved for an elite of Christians who pride themselves on being able "to be grateful that they are not like the rest of the world." In the church there is no such thing as "good people" and "better people." There are no classes among the people of God! Each state and condition of person has its charm and grace. The conjugal experience allows people to discover a certain meaning in life and to live in a certain joy. The experience of virginity allows people to discover the same meaning in life, but in a different way. The same joy, but in a totally different way. It's absolutely ridiculous to set up a contest between virginity and conjugal life. No human being can experience everything. Together, we can have an overall experience of life. The sign of the Kingdom can be given in its full extension only by the Universal Church. It's by sharing the gifts of a people that we can discover the unity of the meaning of life, with some people bearing witness to one part and some to another part. Virginity is a gift from the Spirit, given to certain people as a radical sign of the Kingdom. Because virginity is a gift, an *a priori* link between celibacy and priesthood becomes more and more unthinkable. Celibacy belongs more to those people who respond to the monastic and religious calling. Priesthood, so far as we know, is really a ministry in the service of a people. But that's another story! Now, in the style of a Christmas tale, I prefer giving free rein to meditation, for ultimately, we come to realize we are not really talking about the Virgin. In her presence, we can at best tell ourselves stories that she could tell herself, stories that she could tell her son.

· Mary Is Secondary
For God's Sake!

Knowing I was going to give a talk about the Virgin, a friend confronted me: "You're gonna talk about the Virgin? She's secondary!"

"Well, yes, granted, she's indeed secondary! Especially in our time!" We've really got better things to do than worry about a virgin, even if she's the Mother of God. We've really got too much to do to worry about some insignificant virgin. We've really got too many important people to see, far too many V.I.P. clients, to place any value on secondary people, secondary things:

- Saying hello in the morning because every morning is a new morning is secondary.
- Holding the door for someone who could just as easily go through without our holding the door is secondary.
- Looking up at the sky just to look up at the sky is secondary.
- Setting the table nicely. Doing a careful job of it. Entertaining your friends—it's all secondary.
- And fun and flowers? And music? Aren't they secondary?

By eliminating secondary things, one becomes very primary. God is not primary. God is not sectarian. Why deprive him of the joy he gives us of loving his mother? God did a careful job of it. It's true that when coming to earth, he didn't choose just anyone to be his mother. It's true that this mother who's-not-just-anyone is, nevertheless, quite secondary. I like the Virgin *because* she's secondary. In everything she is, in everything she's not, she tells us: What counts is God! The Virgin has always seconded God.

Mary never had first place. In Bethlehem, she had no place at all. Can you see her at the door of her house? In the stable? In a grotto? You're not quite sure where. Out in the open, probably, for the sake of God, who decided to be born in December—and indeed, why not in August? And then, Mary was always put in her place, a bit like a chambermaid. Mary is a chambermaid's name. We know we're not supposed to say *maid*. That's why traditionally Christian families in France seldom name a girl plain *Marie*. However, since they do like the "Blessed Virgin" all the same, they use Marie as a middle name or in a double name: Jean-Marie, Marie-Thérèse. So don't say you don't like people calling the Virgin secondary. It's useless for Mary to be glorified in the Assumption; she's still not glorious enough for us on earth!

Seeing and Believing
Mary never had first place. Mary was always put in her place. First, by Joseph. Admit that the outset was quite hard. By Jesus himself. In Jerusalem: "Doubt not that I am here to do my Father's work!" At Cana: "My hour has not yet come! This is not the moment!" But we should not be shocked by this kind of apparently harsh retort. Mary *was confident*. She knew that this was surely affection! She knew what her son meant. Without understanding everything, without understanding fully, she discovered day by day, little by little, who her son was. Mary already knew that her place was by the cross. Mary knew quite well that no one could take her place by the cross. But she didn't know it as a prophet would who guesses the future. She knew it as a seer of God. By using the word *seer* I'm not getting into the occult. I mean to describe the almost unbelievable lucidity of luminous faith! Mary's faith is so lucid because she doesn't need her human eyes to have a sense of God, to see the truth.

Mary got on admirably with God. An astonishing seer because she was a happy believer. Mary saw that her place was by the cross. She saw that the cross was the cross of everyday life. Mary saw that the cross of the last day was the cross of days and men! Mary, who had given the light of day to Him who thought only about his "Hour," was there on that Friday, in tears, devastated. But right in her place! In the shadow of the Tree whose roots had been planted in her heart. The cross of her crucified Jesus! He was finally an adult, that Child. The child about whom one always wonders, when it's one's own child, whether he will ever grow up. Here was this child now, very high up: "Father, I place my spirit in your hands." "Mary, I place my body in your hands." She, who had given life to her son, received his death.

The Mother at Home

Here is this mother of God through the ages, going over "all these things preserved in her heart," her pierced heart, as Simeon said, that old man so experienced in the ways of God. She who surveyed her whole life from the viewpoint of Calvary—what had she done with her life, this girl from Galilee?

In regard to Mary's discretion, I can see the people of her village telling one another: "There's a sweet thing living on that narrow sloping street. A sweet charming little thing!" (Charming always means little.) She had an absolutely adorable little boy. Oh how adorable. People just couldn't believe. And Joseph? Old Joseph! But no, not *that* old! Old is affectionate. It's strange, people always depict Mary as very young and soft and Joseph with a beard, a sort of precocious old man. Certainly, Mary did not *know* her husband (in the Biblical sense). But that's no reason to think she married a grandfather! So, little Mary, what were you doing in Nazareth when Joseph was doing his carpentry? If I know her, when she went to draw water, she must have let the old and worthy matrons get to the well first. And then one Thursday (or Wednesday in some countries!), she must have been preparing a nice snack. That's when Jesus saw that they weren't making big cakes that rise very high without yeast! At home, Mary was sewing. There's always some mending to do. That's when Jesus saw that it's silly to place new patches on worn sheets. Mary taught Jesus how to mend.

Mary was a good housewife and mother. You don't say anything about a housewife and mother. As we know, you don't say that a housewife works, you say she has work to do. After twenty centuries, Mary, mother of God, mother of men, is an old, worn-out mother. One would like to place her in a Catholic old-age home. Let's not make too much of a fuss about it! In any case, she shouldn't lack a thing. That's what people always say when they send someone to an old-age home. She's nice and snug with all the saints in paradise. We'll drop by every year! During vacation, it'll give the kids something to do, we'll go to masses August 15, after all, it's a holy day of obligation.

For More Than Four Thousand Years

Old mother of God. Old mother of men. Tender affection. Silence of dawns. How beautiful a beautiful old woman is! I've always noticed that old mothers don't talk anymore. Their smiles do the talking for them. Their eyes light up like embers under wafting ashes. Their eyes tell us that their hearts are immensely young. Mary, old mother who has never grown old. Oh, Mary, Song of Songs, for more than four thousand years! It's wonderful having an old mother with an eternal heart, waiting for you in the New World. An old mother with a prophetic heart. Would you still say that Mary's beauty is secondary? Perhaps. But you will not prevent me from quoting Paul Claudel:

> For being there forever
> Simply for being Mary
> Simply for existing
> Mother of Jesus Christ, I thank you.

9

Jesus of Nazareth, Son of God: Someone Human

Faith Is Something More

His state was divine,
yet he did not cling
to his equality with God
but emptied himself
to assume the condition of a slave,
and became as men are;
and being as all men are,
he was humbler yet,
even to accepting death,
death on a cross.
But God raised him high,
and gave him the Name
which is above all other names
so that all beings
in the heavens, on earth and in the underworld
should bend the knee at the name of Jesus
and that every tongue should acclaim
Jesus Christ as Lord
to the glory of God the Father.

(Philippians 2:6–11)

A Plausible Humanity

Just as Jesus did not try to prove that he was God, so he did not attempt to *prove* that he was human. It was by showing himself as someone human that Christ made his humanity believable. In order to believe in Christ's humanity, we need first to realize that Jesus was a man like us. Like anyone else. So, people list the things of life that Christ experienced and that assure us his humanity was not bogus. People comb the Gospels for actions that make the humanity of the Son of God plausible. A touching enterprise!

· Jesus, an Expert in Humanity
A Man Like Anyone Else

Jesus was marked by the past. He had a heredity. He belonged to a people. He was born in a given country. He lived in a specific era. The Gospel intimates that he was hungry and thirsty. He was tired and he slept. He was moved. And happily moved that Lazarus was raised from the dead. This allows us to say that Jesus wept! Like all men, Jesus had his limits. Having become flesh, having lived among us, he inevitably experienced and wanted to experience the finite. He had to stop every evening. He says so himself: "The night will soon be here when no one can work" (John 9:4). He got up every day. He went to bed. And he started all over again. He couldn't be everywhere at once: Jerusalem, Jericho—he couldn't do everything at once: be in the crowd and pray to his father on the mountain. He couldn't be "nice" to Mary and Joseph and then let them discover that he "had to be about his father's business." Jesus could not live in both the first and the twentieth century at once. He could not be a craftsman, industrialist, and professor— all at once. An only child—and have brothers and sisters. A bachelor and a married man with a family.

You only live once. Christ lived only once. He did not experience what all men can experience in all lives. Very frequently, on the pretext that Jesus' humanity is universal, people conceive of Jesus' life as summing up all human situations. Jesus' life is not a digest of our existences.

But because Christ experienced his humanity as the Son of God, he didn't have to experience all human things to be universal. In a universal way, he can join every single human being in his particularity. Because Christ experienced his humanity through the Spirit that inhabits us all, he experienced inwardly everything that each of us can experience now in a unique way. Jesus is a true human being, not because he assumed the contingencies of the human condition, but rather because he lived with an intensity of life that no other person has ever managed to experience. The most passionate of humanities: that is what Jesus experienced and it qualified him as an expert in humanity.

The few human encounters he managed to have during his lifetime on earth assure us that he was not only able to understand all that is incomprehensible in us; he was also able to communicate to us *his* reasons for living as a human being. With the woman of Samaria, he understood, through the troubled waters of a checkered life, our thirst for the Water of the source. With the rich man, he understood, through this man's desire for perfection, our thirst for the absolute. With the adulteress, he understood the solitude of the condemned. He shows us he is human by telling us not to judge. In his *lapidary* (stonelike) sentence: "Go, sin no more," Jesus upsets all the stones of our mutual stonings in order to make us realize at last that there is only one thirst, the thirst to love. The thirst of human beings. . . .

Jesus the Man: What's His Importance

What sense does it make nowadays to ask ourselves about Christ's humanity? What is the meaning of this question? What is the importance for us today of Jesus the Man?

What we ask of Jesus today is that he make us aware of the Love he knows in his eternal humanity as the Son of God, not that he show us every aspect of his manifestations through the ages. While our human actions are often laughable, while the vanity and vacuity, the emptiness and windiness of our strawlike lives would ultimately rob us of hope, what we ask of Jesus Christ is to make us believe in the importance of Love. Yes, we need to be important. Important with love. This is what reveals Christ's humanity today: Love in the most hollow everyday things is not an added value. Our life has meaning in itself. Christ does not give meaning to our lives. He lets us discover that he himself is the meaning of love. Thus, the thunderous light of the Incarnation has already appeared, the wonder of God's humanity within us. Because God became human, nothing human thereafter could be without godliness. And there will be nothing godly without humanness. The little lark, Saint Joan, soaring in the sun of the Love that consumed her, understood this very clearly. At her trial, the judges tried to make her say that everything she had done was ultimately caused by God alone, who made her do it. But she retorted: "God, yes, Good Lord! Joan with God!" Such is the audacity of faith in the humanity of God.

A Man Unlike Others

Because Jesus is without sin, because the power of the Resurrection is already operating within him, because he is in perfect communion with the Father and the Spirit, Christ is different from us. Christ thus reveals something we can experience for ourselves: Often, the more we differ from others, the better we understand them. It is as much his difference from human beings as his similarity to them that makes Jesus' humanity so likeable. Jesus was alone among men in having a perfectly successful humanity. The blossoming of Christ in his fully successful humanity not only invites us, but also gives us the strength to achieve our human adulthood in Christ. The very fact of knowing that one human being, at least one man on earth, Jesus, succeeded in his life as a human being widens the possibilities of our own humanity. We know that a human being can be humanized. We know that mankind is capable of progress. We know that with Christ we can grow to become more of a person. For his humanity is not just the memory of a great man to emulate, but a comunicable reality; and it is communicable because Christ's humanity today is the humanity of Christ Risen. Christ is not simply a master of thought; he is alive today through the Spirit, who transforms us. Christ gives each of us the chance to become that "other" whom we are called upon to give birth to in order to be ourselves. To believe in Christ's humanity today is ultimately to believe in man. In this way, the faith that gives birth to our lives as human beings is not merely a supplement to the soul, as Henri Bergson would have it. It is really an "interior of the soul." It is a *plus-être*, as Teilhard de Chardin called it: "being something more."

The point is not to discuss Christ's humanity theoretically, but to verify, in our human experience, the full scope of the human experience that God had. What interests us is to discover how Christ's humanity gives our humanity its full measure. While Christ lives his human life passionately, to the ultimate passion of the cross, what passionately interests us today is to know what good it was in the end. Is Sartre right? Is man "a useless passion?"

· The Man Greater Than Man
Man Is Not the Master of Man

Ever since man became man, he has been looking for himself. In this quest for himself, the variations of language aptly express the fluctuations of the idea of man. For centuries, the Western world spoke about "human nature." The French Revolution did not wait to find out what human nature was in order to decree what the "rights of man" should be. Now, so it seems, the rights of man have given way to the right of life. Today, people talk more about the "sacred right of life" and respect for the individual. But just what is man that his life should be sacred? Just what is man, Lord?

The burning question of abortion seems to bring out very lucidly the crisis of our lack of knowledge of man. I bring it up only to stress that in my opinion the first obstacle to the knowledge of God is the lack of knowledge of man. The first obstacle to faith in God is the lack of faith in man. Thus, in regard to the two positions on abortion, I will simply let myself be questioned by the facts, without taking sides.

On the one hand, some physicians favor abortion, and not just in therapeutic instances, of course. In regard to this position, I find it hard to believe that people who devote their lives to making their fellow humans live would advocate abortion frivolously and for want of a sense of the human.

On the other hand, some physicians flatly reject any kind of abortion. They'll do anything to make a life see the light of day whatever the foreseeable setbacks. As a result, babies are born without arms or legs. Here again, I find it hard to believe that people who devote their lives to making life succeed would take such responsibilities heedlessly; just for the sake of a morality that's judged to be obscurantist.

In the case of a traumatizing birth as in the case of a normal one, we can feel on a gut level—without being able to prove it—that a person who could have existed, as soon as the process of life begins, and who does not exist is an abortive, a deficient human being. Deficient not only to himself but to the world.

We obviously must have faith in man to believe that the world cares for us the way we care for the world.

We must have faith in man to believe, whatever our insignificance and our infirmities, in the irreplaceable value of the unique human being that each of us is.

We must have faith in God to believe that God cares so deeply for human beings that he himself became a human being.

We must have faith in God to believe that if we had prevented the Only Begotten Son, the Unique Son, from being this Unique Man, then God himself would not be what he is. The world would not be what it is. We would not be what we are.

Hence, no matter how upsetting the smile of a little baby without arms or legs, no matter how unbearable the tears of a child without arms or legs, no matter how revolting this arbitrary work of the absurd, we sense that a human being is more than his arms and legs. We can then ask ourselves, in light of so many diminished human beings: What does our God tell us today about life, our God who, in Jesus Christ, died with his arms on the cross and his feet pierced?

Jesus Christ spent his life curing people. It was as a healer that Jesus was seen by the masses: a bonesetter, patching up bits of human suffering. Those people took their own good time to realize that in mending the breaks in our bodies, he was mending the breaks in our hearts. And then that same Jesus Christ, as though forgetting the secret tears he shed at mutilated bodies, tells us things that can seem inhuman. Indeed, they go beyond humanity. They take us way beyond what we know about human beings. In a context totally different from disease, Jesus affirms that it is better to enter the Kingdom of heaven with only one eye or one hand than to remain at the gate with all one's parts, but not as a human being who is fully a human being. Naturally, it would be odious—and that's not our aim—to justify inexplicable human suffering in some stupidly conciliatory way with an ill-timed quotation from the Gospels. Here, as elsewhere,

here as always, Jesus, by the manner in which he lived his humanity, asks us to believe that man is greater than men. Jesus always sees further than things that appear so far to us. He simply tells us: "Have a higher idea of man than what you think you know about his happiness. You are worth more than a sparrow. Don't be superficial. Don't worry about your clothes. Go further than the satisfaction of having clothes that look nice. You are more beautiful than your beauty. More intelligent than your intelligence. Better than the best among you. You are inhabited by Someone all consuming: the Spirit. It is the Spirit who makes you understand that you are not your own point of reference." Man is not the master of man. Jesus of Nazareth reveals to us that the mystery of man is the mystery of God in man. The mystery of God makes man, as Saint Paul explains to the Philippians.

The Happiness of God Is the Greatness of Man

It is good to meditate on Christ's humanity in the light of the great, fundamental text of Christian faith quoted at the beginning of this chapter. It is a hymn—one of the very first in the early church—that the Christian communities sang when exalting their burgeoning faith.

Too bad that many people see Christ's humanity only as a device of God's to restore his work of creation, which had been degraded by sin. As though God's humanity were a device!

I have always been struck by the simplistic shortcuts used by the catechesists to explicate the passage from sin to salvation. They seem to view it as an automatism foreseen through all eternity. First era: Man, created by love, rejects God's love; this is sin. Second era: God so loves the world that he sends his Son; this is salvation. One thus coldly speaks of God's love as if it were a motor beginning a process to which one ultimately remains quite exterior. One speaks of Christ's incarnation as though it were a forced emergency repair that cost God dearly. When man fell, he fell very low. How can he be taken out of the pit of sin without an expert in human depths? God is viewed as a sort of master sumpman, condescending to let his Son descend to earth! Thus, when we closely examine the vocabulary of our old Christmas carols, we find it celebrates God's self-humbling; we also note that Jesus Christ's humanity is conceived of as a sort of obligation that God inflicts upon himself.

So, to thank God for this condescension, man, apparently, can come up with nothing better than to grovel in protestations of unworthiness. We tend to acknowledge God's "merit" in humbling himself to become human rather than his joy in elevating us in his happiness. I have never heard anyone say that God was happy to become a human being. To forget that God's happiness is made of this greatness in being human is to go along with an atheism that rightly rejects a God who made himself human because he had no choice. If one fails to realize that, for God, Jesus Christ is the desired Child, the awaited Child, the desired Man, the Man of his dreams, in whom he was well pleased, in whom he finds his joy, then one cannot believe that God's glory is man fully human in Jesus Christ.

God's No Skinflint

To become human was a richness for God. Certainly, man adds nothing to God. Precisely because God doesn't have to be enriched from the outside; when he becomes man, one can be truly certain that he draws this richness from his own capital. The captivating thing about Christianity is to discover that man is so much a part of God that God cannot do without man. God loves man jealously. I don't think we can vitally believe that God loves us so long as we have not tasted God's jealousy. Yes, our God is a jealous God. Jealous not in the sense of touchy or envious, of course. Jealous in the sense that he is captivated by everything affecting man.

It is in this light that we must understand the line, "God did not cling jealously to his equality with God." This is a paraphrase that tries to render, after a fashion, a precise Greek word, which I now offer in a verbatim image: "God was no skinflint." Our jealous God was not a God who was miserly about his wealth as the Son of God, miserly about his titles and perogatives. He, who was of divine condition, never presumed on it. He never thought he was falling from a high estate when he became human; and yet, Saint Paul does say that God lowered himself by becoming flesh: "Being as all men are, he was humbler yet, even to accepting death, death on a cross."

The humiliation for God doesn't consist in agreeing to "grow small" in order to become human. Nor in being placed on the level of the small and spending his time with the small. One totally misunderstands the Gospel if one views Christ's predilection for the small as humiliation. The humiliation for God is not so much embracing the human condition as assuming the human condition of *sinners*. He who was without sin took sin upon himself. He was fettered by sin, like a slave, but he was freed by the Resurrection to become the perfectly free man. That's why "God raised him high, and gave him the name which is above all other names." And this exaltation of the Son of God becomes, in Jesus Christ Risen, the exaltation of man. At Christmas, when we celebrate the arrival of God in our humanity, our joy is twofold: it extols both the wonder of our human preferment and God's eternal gladness at being human. But who, on the night of the Nativity, rejoices spontaneously in God's happiness about living as a human being twenty centuries ago, and being, in the midst of the men of this century, the Son of God, everlastingly human?

• The Four Cardinal Points

What about Christ's humanity today, among us? I once tried to get a precise idea of what Christ would talk about today, if he had to give a new Sermon on the Mount, for instance in Times Square or the Place de la Concorde. Chatting with a group of young people (eighteen-to twenty-five-year-olds), I said: "Suppose Christ gave a huge press conference that was telecast all over the world. Assume you could only ask him four questions. What, in your opinion, are the four cardinal points that define man today and that Christ would have something to say about?" With some slight variations they agreed unanimously on: money, sex, politics, and drugs. Nothing new under the sun, you say. However, these four words are reference points, aptly describing the horizon of a crowd of people, a people facing the human realities of our time.

Money

They could have spoken of social success, career advancement, "being able to do what you like." But the term *money* is more precise. What counts is having money. Having money is having the respectability of the man who pays cash, the customer's right over everyone else.

What is Jesus' drift when he declares: "One cannot serve two masters at once: God and Mammon"? No more and no less than one cannot "have" and "be." This distinction between "having" and "being" is a commonplace, which we must remember all the more precisely because it *is* common. The common is most commonly forgotten by most people! Your money increases your "having" and reduces your "being"! To serve Mammon is to give priority to having over being. Being is the desire of a few young people who prefer living to owning. How horrified and scandalized their families are when they casually announce that they're going off on vacation without reserving a hotel room. They buy a stereo before they buy a kitchen table! After all, they're reminding us that man is also musical. Christ, it seems, does not moralize like the fabled parsimonious ant. He's more on the cricket's side. He talks about birds that do not sow or reap. He whispers in our ears with his own music: "Sing a little more now, and some day you'll dance for joy!" Stop buying in the illusion that you're amassing things for your kids. Gather treasures in heaven; there are no moths or worms there to eat up your goods. You're worth more than your pennies! Some day, you will no longer shine with your savings in the eyes of the world. You've counted so much, but you won't be able to count on your savings. Don't say you're buying a country house to free you from the city if you become a slave to your house. When I say "country house," it's only a symbol. Everyone buys his or her castles in Spain, wherever possible. I am simply referring to the dreadful kind of property owner who grows old before his time. But I also realize it's very hard to possess as though *not* possessing.

"Yes, gather treasures in heaven; there are no moths or worms there." Christ does not scorn the goods of this world. He simply advocates the wisdom of soaring, of seeing things as relative, of detaching oneself. True, Christ had a great thing going. No family to take care of. No budget to cope with. No company committees to direct. No income-tax installment to pay. No archbishop's palace to build. Christ doesn't reproach us for being tied to a world in which money talks. He, who spoke of talents and lauded the resourceful steward, asks the Christian to be spiritually cunning and profit evangelically from the world in which he is incarnated. He asks us to invest our lives according to the hierarchy of values that he reveals to us. So what values will you bet on? Stocks or beatitudes? A simplistic stance is no longer appropriate. That's not quite the way to ask the question, for Jesus never opposed Caesar to God: "Give Caesar what is Caesar's and God what is God's." Doesn't Caesar, too, belong to God?

Sex

To talk of sex when one would talk of eroticism reveals the powerful force of sex which rules both minds and bodies. Indeed, the attraction of sex is at least a sign of both moral decadence and the spiritual *angst* of man seeking the Other.

To speak of sex when one feels like speaking of love reveals the present-day materialism of the love we idolize. Saint Paul said about his contemporaries: "Their God is their belly." If he returned to earth today, he would no doubt say: "Their sex is their God!"

To speak of sex when one would rather speak of the meaning of human sexuality in love is, ultimately, to wonder about the meaning of the human condition, a sexual condition. What does our God of Love in Jesus Christ, who became human, have to tell us? For if Christ fully assumed the human condition, we may ask how he assumed the sexual condition in his life as a human being. This is all the more intriguing because of his singular condition—celibacy. Paradoxically, it is this practical and not theoretical celibacy that speaks of its own accord. Indeed, Christ gives no speech; but the vital equilibrium he evinces supports the possibility of integrating sexuality beyond the sexual relation. There's nothing else to say. Christ reveals to us that sexuality is more fundamental than the sexual act. Sexuality is a totality. It is not everything. If the equilibrium in human life is conditioned by sexual equilibrium, then Christ reveals to us that beyond carnal mediation there is a source of love that is expressed through an equivalent potential of giving and receiving, that is, in a universal availability. Christ thus places our lives in their dimension of eternity.

He proclaims that in the kingdom to come (its reality is present because it is already here) there shall be neither man nor woman. This *doesn't* imply that sexual relations are bad per se (a belief that has prevailed in some cultures for centuries). On the contrary, they express a communion so intimate that Christ himself chose marriage as the sign of his own union with mankind. However, Jesus, fully human without having known sexual sharing, draws our attention to the problems of communicability and the limits of sexuality in encounters between human beings. In fact, while sexuality tends to achieve the perfect rapport of two people in one flesh—a single togetherness—it also permits us to experience, within the most overwhelming intimacy, an unslaked void, a basic incompleteness, a metaphysical isolation, in the desire for Something else.

Politics

Time was when people spoke of man as a "social being." Today, they tend to speak more of a man as a "political being." Indeed, the relations among people seem more and more affected by the political dimension, and so deeply that certain Christians make politics a *sine qua non* of faith. Politics, in the etymological sense of the word, expresses at once the solidarity and combativeness of men fighting to build the city (*polis*). Christ, by the way he placed himself in the world, which was his, seems both committed and noncommitted. Committed, not in the sense of making a pledge, joining a party. But rather committed in the sense of being in the thick of the society of his era, a society he did not choose. Tied to the mores of his time, he accepts the customs of his people: he was circumcised, he was presented in the temple. Yet this solidarity with the people of his time, while indicating a concrete attachment to what constitutes the best in their lives, also manifests a refusal to rubber stamp everything that encloses them in their sectarianism.

Christ, awaited as the Messiah who was supposed to restore political self-determination in Israel, refuses to view "politics" as a condition for announcing the Kingdom. Christ refuses the kind of reasoning that argues: first clean up the political situation, then we'll proclaim the Gospel. It's true that the political situation must be cleaned up. But the Gospel won't wait. We can rejoice at seeing Christians no longer scorning politics—which some call "corrupt"—we can rejoice at the serious commitment of so many Christians who do not wish to live their faith in a disincarnate manner. But still and all, we cannot go along with the politically polarized, who regard politics as an absolute. Here, too, Christ keeps his distance. One constantly notices in him a dialectics of communion and rupture. Taking sides, he is not partisan. Conforming to the rules of Israel, he is not conformist. Consistent with the law, he is not legalistic. Attached to tradition, he is not traditionalist. He respects tradition, but he also flies in its face; for instance, when the sabbath becomes an institution that serves man. He is not conservative, but he is not revolutionary either. Or rather, yes he *is*: but his is the revolution of love, the revolution of the radical change brought about by love. If we must speak of revolution, then the only revolution that Christ actually experienced was the passage from death to life.

Drugs

One could speak of LSD or hash. Drugs, quite plainly, are not just the lot of a few. Every person knows his own inability to really change, to become totally different; and at the same time, every person knows the way in which he tries to escape to somewhere else. Drugs are an escape from oneself. Christ, by his way of being present to himself, stops us from seeking what's best about ourselves anywhere but within ourselves. In this way, Christ's humanity, contemplated, loved, imitated, is the source of life for people today.

With a Human Love

Because Christ loved all that God could love with a human love,

Because Christ named all that God could name with a human name,

Because Christ, Firstborn of Creation, is the Eldest of a flock of brothers,

> truly all Creation
> on earth as in heaven
> exults joyously
> at the name of Jesus:
> Jesus the Man
> Jesus the God

Jesus of Nazareth, only betotten son of Mary and Joseph Jesus, the Word, the Only Begotten Son of the Father in the Spirit

> God of God
> True God of true God
> Man of men
> True man of true men
> JESUS CHRIST

10

Jesus: Someone We Can't Do Without

Faith Saves

Have mercy on me, O God, in your goodness,
in your great tenderness wipe away my faults,
wash me clean of my guilt,
purify me from my sin.

For I am well aware of my faults,
I have my sin constantly in mind,
having sinned against none other than you,
having done what you regard as wrong.

You are just when you pass sentence on me,
blameless when you give judgment.
You know I was born guilty,
a sinner from the moment of conception.

Yet, since you love sincerity of heart,
teach me the secrets of wisdom.
Purify me with hyssop until I am clean;
wash me until I am whiter than snow.

Instill some joy and gladness into me,
let the bones you have crushed rejoice again.

Hide your face from my sins,
wipe out all my guilt.

God, create a clean heart in me
put into me a new and constant spirit;
do not banish me from your presence,
do not deprive me of your holy spirit.

Be my savior again, renew my joy,
keep my spirit steady and willing;
and I shall teach transgressors the way to you,
and to you the sinners will return.

Save me from death, God my savior,
and my tongue will acclaim your righteousness;
Lord, open my lips,
and my mouth will speak out your praise.
                                      (Psalm 51)

Light the Light!

> I was born guilty,
> A sinner from the moment of conception.
> I have my sin constantly in mind.

The lamentations of Psalm 51 are ascribed to King David
after his murderous deed. David desired Bathsheba, wife of
Uriah, his chief general. Taking advantage of a perilous
battle, the king sent his rival to the front lines. And indeed,
Uriah was killed in a blaze of glory. Naturally, he will have
military honors. The crime is clean, but David drags his
heart in the mud. His sin remains before him, an indelible
blemish. He understands that the evil is within him. "I was
born guilty." His enormous crime has ramifications in his
heart. It is not an isolated act. It is like those treacherous
reefs whose tips emerge from the sea, making us forget the
archipelagoes under the surface. This crime is steeped in
egoism, pride, sensuality, wickedness. Making himself the

center of his being, David excludes the other. The other is an intruder: this is egoism. Using his power, he dominates; the other is the inferior: this is pride. Allowing the field of his desire to be invaded by covetousness, he enjoys the other; the other is his object: this is sensuality. Stifling in his heart what is best about himself, he destroys the other. He himself is wiped out. He no longer recognizes himself. Blindness is the insidious root of wickedness. It is then that the prophet Nathan reveals to David: "You are this man." The prophet's words, as dazzling as a sudden blaze in the night, strike us fully in the face. Each one of us. The egoism, pride, sensuality, wickedness hidden away in the backs of the closets of the heart come to take up so much space that they ultimately overflow the closets and occupy the entire apartment. We no longer recognize ourselves in the clutter of furniture. Take a good look. "Light the light. You are this man!"

• The Possessed
The Rebel

Man, to be sure, is not reduced to being only the "sewer of iniquity," as Pascal suggested. Nor is he a candid little creature to whom is given "the Good Lord without a confession," as Rousseau would have it. Between Pascal's pessimism and Rousseau's optimism, there is a place for man, "the original sinner, saved before all origin." It would be morbid to lock oneself up in this black universe of guilt; and likewise, it would be naive to see everything through rose-colored glasses. We savor the finest things in life like invalids who appreciate the sun of Existence all the more because they walk with the tenacity of people who suffer. We are sickened with sin. An incurable disease. "I was born guilty." I feel sick. I'm sick. I feel bad. I'm bad. Wretched about being bad.

Being bad is different from feeling bad. When you say, "I feel bad, sick." The bad pain is generally localized: your arm feels bad; it hurts when you bend it. Like cancer, the localized pain spreads rapidly. Eventually, the entire body feels bad. When I do something bad, I not only commit a sin, I discover that I am a sinner. Ultimately, one could say: there is no such thing as sin, there are only sinners. Sin is more radical than the act of sinning. It reveals a condition of primal poverty, congenital frailty. Sin is more serious than sins. That is why the great saints confessed every day. Saints are people who, being in a love relationship with God, know that to sin is not just to commit an infraction positively, but to refuse to be in a relationship of gratuitous love with God. To refuse to be what one is uniquely. Committing a lot of sins is not what makes you more of a sinner; refraining from committing a lot of sins is not what keeps you from being a big sinner!

One must "do with" this condition of sinner. The "must" is heavy with the fatefulness that made André Gide say tragically: "Sinning is something I cannot help doing." Since man strives for freedom, where does that troubling propensity come from, his propensity for locking himself up? Since man strives for love, justice, peace, where does that strange heredity come from, the heredity of harshness that he has been dragging along for centuries? Even at his mother's breast, the innocent baby already has the seeds of hatred and violence in him. Where does this mysterious human attraction come from, this attraction to the least good thing about oneself? Where does this inability come from, this inability to *want* thoroughly what one *desires* profoundly? Gide's cry merely repeats Saint Paul's: "The good I would like to do I do not do, and the evil I would not like to do, I do...."

Ultimately, why is man not master of himself? Because of original sin? Yes, certainly; but the last word about it hasn't

been said. Admittedly, the evils of poverty, war, social injustice, racism, hunger in the world may in part be the collective consequence of sin in the world. But what about the
cataclysms that intensify poverty? And the catastrophes
that cause famine? Not to mention: boredom, loneliness,
ugliness, stupidity, deformity in people and objects, the
things that are senseless and nonsensical in human existence. To what extent are we responsible?

If we are to distinguish between evil and sin, then perhaps we should try to do so on the level of responsiblity. Evil
would be more indeterminate, more confused, even more
mysterious than sin. One could say that evil is less dependent on us than sin: we are not responsible for cataclysms.
But what about war? Is it really worth making distinctions?
After all, in the final analysis, people will tell us—without
being able to explain it—we are all, invisibly, indirectly,
responsible for the evil that occurs in the world. Evil appeared in the world "through the fault of one man." Scripture ultimately doesn't distinguish between evil and sin.
The distinction is made in regard to the notion of fault, of
blame, which implies responsiblity. "Sin entered the world
through the fault of one man, and through sin, death," says
Saint Paul (Romans 5:12). That was original sin. Death and
sin go hand in hand, because, according to the philosophers, death, like evil, is "non-being." To say that evil is
"non-being" doesn't mean it doesn't exist: it simply means
that, on a philosophical level, it has no substance. In everyday life, whether evil is "non-being" or isn't "non-being,"
we are often overwhelmed by its fatefulness. This heredity
of evil has never been truly justified, and certain people
revolt against it. This revolt may seem naive. We feel the
sense of injustice that one feels in regard to collective
punishment. One student gets out of line, and the whole
class is in for it! One man sinned, and all mankind is condemned! Nevertheless, the famous "one man" that the Bi-

ble speaks of can't possibly be Adam alone. "I too am that man!"

The story of Adam and Eve strikes us an antiquated. And yet—this is what annoys us—one can't blot it out of the history of the world. Every human being is a world. Every time a human being is born, this is creation for him. Every time a human being dies, this is the end of the world for him. Every human being is the first human being. What's so amazing, then, if each human being finds within him- or herself the mysterious origin. It's traumatic for a child not to know where he comes from. Man wants to know where he comes from. The man blind from birth wants to know where his night of sin comes from. The first man sinned; but who existed before him? The French bishops convening at Lourdes in 1972 said: "The Christian knows that evil comes from far away. Sin smashes the world." It's too easy to say that evil exists in man's heart. Why is it there? Where *does* it come from?

From someone? But why insist that evil exists personally? The Devil? Isn't that a diabolical idea that man pathologically comes up with by himself? What does it really matter if evil comes from someone or something? Aren't we all entangled just the same? So why do we want the Devil to exist?

Christianity is not an ideology. The way we try to account for the existence of evil is not the result of an intellectual system, it is the welcoming of Revelation. There is no abstract truth in Christianity. The Revelation teaches us that evil is not an idea, it is someone. In effect, we must recognize that we change nothing about the facts by saying that evil is someone or something. But on the level of the notion we may have of God when dealing with evil, this statement can change everything. On this level, it is worth asking whether evil is something or someone. If one speaks of evil as an abstract reality, then, I think, one feels the objections of a certain style of intellectual atheism identified with Albert Camus. Camus rejects God—not theoretically, but on this precise point: God allows evil to operate. If evil is only a principle, then God is responsible for it. It is understandable that a man can reject a God who allows evil to operate. If evil is someone, a demon, one can accept the fact that God "allows someone to operate," for God does not oppose the freedom of his creatures. But one cannot put up with his allowing "something" to operate if it derives directly from his freedom. It remains to be seen how God's freedom operates in regard to this someone.

The Fallen Angel

During a public audience in November 1971, Pope Paul VI recalled "the aggressive power of the demon and the sinister action of the disturber of man's equilibrium. Satan is public enemy number one. He sneaks in through deviations that are both harmful and seemingly consistent with our mental structures or our deepest aspirations."

This is certainly the ruse of the person whom the Bible calls the Father of lies. The Evil One would like to make us believe that the depth of the human being is open to influences that are merely anarchic impulses having nothing to do with evil. One needn't be well versed in the nooks and crannies of the human heart to realize that so many personalized temptations are directed by an invisible power. It is simplistic to say: "Evil comes only from man," and it is equally simplistic to claim: "There is no seed of evil in man." One cannot explain everything with depth analysis and reduce evil to "complexes" from which one must free oneself in order to be free of the idea of evil! Paul VI cautions us against this egoistical skepticism of people, who, afraid of being thought superstitious, deny the existence of the devil. One mustn't get smart with the devil. It is difficult to talk about a demon; even more difficult, considering what Baudelaire said: "Satan's ruse is to make us think that he doesn't exist." André Gide added: "If the devil could, he would say: I am he who isn't!" Nobody knows who Satan is except perhaps the diabolists who make a pact with him. The diabolists exist. Satan is not a myth.

The Christian, who, on the day of his baptism, says no to the spirit of evil, professes his belief in the existence of the demon. Why not believe in the demon, since so many non-believers are willing to accept the existence of extraterrestrial beings? Why not believe in other beings besides God and man? In this light, the existence of angels is extremely important. Here, too, of course, we must shed those saccharine images of puny creatures with big wings; however, let's not lose sight of how important their existence is! They assure us that creation is vaster than what we can know and God's design even more mysterious than the mystery he reveals to us.

Satan is a rebellious angel. An angel who fell because he was disappointed at having a rival. Not God, but man. Satan saw red when he discovered man's greatness in the eyes of God. Lucifer became infernal for man. He couldn't place above himself the fact that God was pleased with man. Satan directs his aggressions at man in order to wound God. Satan, like the other creatures, is *freedom created*. He therefore can't get the best of God, who is the Creator, *freedom uncreated*. Satan realizes that the Lord his God is not to be tempted. That's why Satan waited for God to become man in Jesus Christ in order to slither again. Because he knows that man rebels against evil, the Slitherer's most insidious way to sting man to the quick is to cultivate evil. Thus, he makes it seem as if evil comes either from God or from man. In any event, Satan wins on both counts. If evil comes from God, man rejects his wretched God. If evil comes from man, man rejects himself. We are caught in a double bind; for—let's state it once again—if man rejects himself, he rejects God. If man can no longer believe in himself, he can no longer believe in God.

God Paralyzed

In regard to Satan, God is impotent, God does not walk with Satan. However, God would no longer be God if he didn't respect the freedom of his creatures. God respects the freedom of Satan, whom he created and who still comes from him, the Lord of all freedom. As if to prove that he takes this created freedom seriously, God accepts the fact that his Kingdom has a parasite. When Jesus teaches us: "Your Kingdom come," it is God himself, in a certain way, who prays, wondering what is happening. To be sure, Satan is not the master of the world, because the Risen Christ came back victorious from death and sin. We are told as much in the highly colorful language of the Revelation: "War broke out in heaven, when Michael with his angels attacked the dragon. The dragon fought back with his angels, but they were defeated and driven out of heaven. The great dragon, the primeval serpent, known as the devil of Satan, who had deceived all the world, was hurled down to the earth and his angels were hurled down with him" (Revelation 12:7–10).

It's thus aberrant to see the demon everywhere. Saint Theresa of Avila was right: "I don't understand these fears that make us say, 'The demon, the demon!' when we can say 'God! God!'" Every time something goes wrong, it doesn't have to be thought of as a "prick of the devil's pitchfork" as the Curé d'Ars put it. And I recall the words of Odette Thibault in *Témoignage Chrétien* (Christian Testimony). "I'm perfectly willing to believe in the Devil so long as he's not just a good excuse, a convenient alibi, a way of dodging our responsibilities."

So much for that: Satan is still the Prince of this world. The evidence speaks for itself! Why wouldn't God be disconcerted by evil? God doesn't want evil. People tend to say: "God doesn't permit it, he simply tolerates it." A nicety that satisfies no one! Because in practice, it boils down to the same thing. No; it may be better to admit what we celebrate on Christmas Eve: we worship our Almighty God in the frailty of the Child. Our strong God is vulnerable.

God himself experiences what he subsequently reveals to Saint Paul: "It's when I'm weak that I'm strong." This "weakness/strength" dialectic is something that God experiences in Jesus Christ, who offers himself up as a victim of evil. God takes Satan at his arguments, but he isn't *taken in* by his game. A victim in fact, God voluntarily becomes a "victim of propitiation," as the Gospel phrases it—that is, favorable for forgiveness.

• The Just
God Only Justifies Man

Because of this specialist of evil, it was necessary that God himself come. Salvation is not merely the restoration of superficial disrepair. Sin attacks the core of the human condition. Salvation is not a simple improvement of the human race, a contribution from God so that man may rehabilitate himself. Salvation is not only an extra chance given to man to make a fresh start. Salvation is re-creation. God alone can create and recreate. That's why Saint Peter preaches, "There is no salvation except in Jesus Christ" (Acts 2). Saint Paul takes up this fundamental revelation of Christianity in a different way. He speaks of God's justice: "God makes his justice known for the present age . . . by showing positively that he is just, and that he justifies everyone who believes in Jesus" (Romans 3:25–26). The faith that saves is the reception of this justice. In the Gospel, salvation and jus tice are synonymous. Justice should not, of course, be taken in the judicial sense. Justifying the sinner doesn't mean exculpating or even acquitting him. When a condemned man is acquitted, he must then get along on his own, "redo his life," as best he can with his criminal record. To justify, for God, is to communicate his justice, that is, his own holiness, which is Love; it means recreating, renewing, converting.

The justified world is the sanctified World. The rectified World. The world in which all the twisted people of the earth can live in the truth and righteousness of the Spirit. Not only those who have sought God with an upright heart, as the liturgy of the mass has us say! As though the Kingdom were not the courtyard of miracles in which those who are maimed in body and mind have priority over all those who imagine they walk straight. It is too bad that the words most apt to help us penetrate the mystery of salvation should have aged so badly. The term *justification*, so often used by Saint Paul in the Letter to the Romans, has lost the richness of its original meaning. Yet, ultimately, it is the only word that can make us grasp what salvation is: God's gift to us of his newness. He makes us new men capable of a new freedom.

The faith that saves is recognition of this gift of freedom. Man is asked to recognize that he is not free, he is simply capable of being freed. Freed by him who is absolute Freedom: the Savior.

The faith that saves us thus expressed by the remission of our misery in God's heart. Mercy is the most ardent manifestation of God's salvation. The word *mercy* is also worn out and may seem assuaging. In fact, it reveals that God alone can cope with sin. "Mercy for every sin." To live in mercy is to admit that, if sin is stronger than man, Jesus Christ is stronger than sin. Taken theoretically, this obvious fact won't change very much in our lives. One can't help agreeing with it. Verified by life, this obvious fact can change everything. The instant one stops viewing sin as an irremovable blemish, one begins to see it as the summons of him who would free us. This is Hope.

The faith that saves is hope. Hope that does not deny ambiguity, for man remains both sinful and saved at the same time. Painful hope, for it can be felt subjectively as duplicity. The Saved Man who lives as a sinner is inclined to feel like something of a hypocrite. We must admit that one feels the weight of sin more heavily than the reality of salvation. One then tends to try to justify oneself.

Man Does Not Justify Himself
There's nothing more human than the need to justify oneself. It's as old as the world. Just look at what Adam says after the fall: "It wasn't me, it was her." Eve is a little cleverer. She doesn't say: "It was him." After all, she could say: "All he had to do was say no." But she has to wriggle out of it all the same. She, too, looks for an expedient. She blames the serpent. All we have are the excuses we find and the reasons we come up with. To justify oneself is to look for extenuating circumstances, excuses that let one admit one might have been wrong. To justify oneself is to look for reasons to be right. And then, also, the true reasons for being truly right. The process of justification involves a movement of self-exoneration, but not of reconciliation with oneself and others. This need for justification shows that man cannot endure living in conflict with himself, in conflict with others. Saint Paul's words "Let yourselves be reconciled," touch upon something very deep in man. One cannot live if one cannot bear the sight of others. One cannot live if one says: "I can't bear the sight of him." Even less if "he" is oneself.

The faith that saves is that of believing more in God's love than in the gravity of one's sin. It means accepting one's inability to get out of sin by oneself, and it also means trying to get out by oneself in order to put oneself in the hands of him who reveals to us that man is the original sinner and yet saved before all beginnings. The first is not Adam but Christ. The first is not man but God. The first is not sin but salvation. If there is a heredity of sin, this doesn't mean that there is a determinism of evil. If man is the object of reprobation, he is still the subject of love for God.

A world closed off to salvation is ultimately a world that refuses to forgive or be forgiven. It is a world unable to believe that God receives all the world and everyone in it. It is a world that dares not create a New World. Salvation is essentially a New World.

The New World! Not only for tomorrow! The New World for today! The church can make the newness of this saved world believable only by its capacity to renew itself and its way of life. The question that then remains to be asked is a raw and bleeding one.

· The Damned
The Church, a Sign of Salvation

In 1971, the French bishops, in a plenary meeting, reaffirmed the church's essential reason for existence: "It is a sign of Salvation in the midst of men." On the level of principles, we may congratulate ourselves on such open and generous statements of intention. On the level of action, are we ready to carry out the concrete demands implied by such declarations? When it comes to facts, we are forced to note a flagrant contradiction between the statement "The Church is a sign of universal salvation," and the present status of people who, having divorced and remarried, are told: "You are not allowed to receive the sacraments." The very sacraments that are signs of universal salvation! I touch on this issue in passing, not in order to deal with something that deserves a much fuller treatment. I simply wish to verify in terms of a precise point how the church visibly realizes inside its structures what it claims to announce outside, to the world.

It would obviously be simplistic not to acknowledge the complexity of this issue. It cannot be resolved easily. What do well-meaning church members say to people who have divorced and remarried? "We painfully share your spiritual suffering. We have taken your case into consideration, and understand how great your pain is. . . ." Words, words, words. Too soft for realities that are hard indeed. We cannot reproach the authorities for seeing far and doing little. The church is caught in its own doctrinal trap.

In its *individual* encounter with people, the church is quite disposed to be as understanding as possible. But in its public life, the reintegration of divorced people who have remarried affects the church in its internal logic, in its doctrinal coherence. In terms of dogma, the church can do nothing but what is dictated by its theological computer. The coherence of dogma is such that one cannot make the slightest inroad without unbalancing the entire body of doctrine. Now, faced with present-day life, the urgency of new situations, the evolution of society, the computer's answers no longer correspond to the questions asked by individuals. We must therefore acknowledge that the church is blocked on this precise issue of the theology of marriage. One cannot get out of an imperturbable logic: the sacrament of marriage signifies that God's Marriage is indissoluble. To agree to smash this sign is tantamount to saying: God's marriage to human beings is not indefectible! Why demand that married people be without defects in the testimony that they try to give to this mystery, since the same intransigence is not shown towards priests who feel they have to leave the ministry and "are admitted to the sacrament of marriage." Isn't the priest, too, a sign of indefectible marriage? We can rejoice that the church doesn't "quarantine" priests who recognize the failure and error in their lives. Let's hope that the church will some day be as receptive to Roman Catholics who have divorced and remarried.

It is not the correctness of this theology that is being challenged, but its functioning. It no longer works. So, are we going to save a theology that has its truth in itself or save the people who are inconsistent with the truth of this theology? It would be futile to oppose the objective truth of theology to the subject truth of people. Theology has a truth in order to link up with the truth of people. But when there is a conflict between theology and people, what would be better: to redo theology or to lose the people who are outside the truth of theology? The church is the master of theology. It can always "develop" dogma. That is, stimulated by the discovery of new times, it can discover new aspects. It waited until the seventeenth century to require the presence of a priest for the validity of a marriage celebration. Taking account of people, one might possibly admit now that the church's acceptance of the remarriage of divorced Catholics is not incompatible with the Eucharist. For, after all, isn't the Eucharist celebrated "in remission of sins"! If it's sinful to remarry, then the Eucharist must be understood as a "remission of sins"! Theology can't be faulted for taking its time to see clearly, but it's hard to put up with having people die without light in the darkness. When we realize how many men, how many women have been crushed, we say: "Too many tears bruise the heart. Too many tears, they kill us in the end. . . . You only live once. You don't have time to wait for councils!" So, if, above all, theology has to be safe today, what else can we say to divorced people who have remarried? "Every man for himself!" But how sad for the church! How dismal to be forced to say: "Too bad for the church," but don't stop loving it all the same! How agonizing to see the church forcing these remarried people not to be able to count on it!

Obviously, there is still Jesus Christ. But in an era when people talk on and on about the church as a sacrament, as the necessary mediation between man and God, the church insists on telling these remarried people: "Get along on your own!" The church is saying the opposite of what it professes theoretically. It is denying itself, because it is admitting in practice that its reason for existence has no reason for existence! I hope that the realization of this lack of logic will open new doors to theology.

"For Every Sin: Mercy!"

The present-day disciplining of people who have divorced and remarried is an avowal of of impotence. For the church cannot both call itself the sign of universal salvation and admit that within its structure there are men and women with the status of being damned.

"For every sin: mercy." How could the world believe this when the most human facts seem to contradict it?

The church appears willing to forgive all sins but those that check it within its structures and strike at its theology; in other words, all sins but those that challenge it in its system. The church is willing to forgive any treason that does not strike at its system; but it is unwilling to forgive two people who recognize the failure of their first marriage and ask the church to assume their failure as its own. Was Isaiah right? "It was our illnesses that Christ bore, it was our sins, our failures." Why shouldn't the church, the sign of Christ, bear all our miseries itself? The terrible thing is that the church gives the impression of fearing failure and its consequences more than sin itself.

True, when refusing the sacraments to people who have divorced and remarried, the church specifies that it doesn't reject them from the mystery of salvation. It doesn't say that such people are not saved. It doesn't even say that they don't have a "certain place" as practicing Christians in the community. It no longer dares to equate them with public sinners. But in fact, since these people continue to be *treated* as public sinners, the world does not place great value on the nice distinctions we can make between the sacramental signs of salvation and the reality of the mystery. The times of niceties is over. These people are accused of hypocrisy, no more and no less. So then why maintain this discipline?

Is the church afraid that a favorable disposition towards remarried divorced people will open the door to all sorts of laxities? The church is afraid that Christians will lower the grandeur of the sacrament of marriage. It's afraid that Christians will do as they like. But what does it think Christians are? Admittedly, not all Christians are at the same point, and the church's qualms are obviously reenforced by our own slowness in changing our ways of thinking. Considering the propriety of the self-righteous, the virtuous demands of second-guessers, the hue and cry of the weak, the church has any number of reasons not to hurry. Its fear expresses our anxieties. Its timidity, our cowardice. To vary Isaiah's words, we may say: "It's our sin that the church bears." But this is no reason to make those involved endure it.

No Discrimination

It is often argued that the church is obliged to maintain an odious stance toward those who remarry because of the bad example they could set. In a human society, such reasonings and blind laws exist, conceivably, to preserve an established order. The law is the law. To break a law is to condemn oneself to exclusion from society. But when the church as a society is made up of members who call themselves and one another brothers, then it doesn't appear in keeping with the morals of the Gospel to have the same criteria of social acceptance and rejection as the rest of the world. If we reject brothers because socially "they are outside the norms" and a source of scandal, aren't we going against Christ the Savior? Didn't he himself reveal salvation while fighting against all kinds of sectarianism and discrimination? This was sharply pointed out by a theologian whom one can hardly call revolutionary: Father Yves Congar (*Le Monde*, December 3–4, 1972): "One of the most striking features of the Gospel, indeed a part of the Messiah Savior's function of setting free, is that Jesus endlessly reintegrates into the community of men and of the faithful those who were excluded for belonging to a category discriminated from the rest: publicans, collectors of tax for the occupation authorities; the adulteress about to be stoned; Mary Magdalene; the Samaritans, a mixed race banned from Jewish society; lepers, impure and hence excluded from public worship.... One could easily place other, more topical words behind those of the Gospel. The mission to liberate remains. It is incumbent upon the entire church, nay, upon the entire human community."

Yes, this mission to liberate is incumbent upon all of us. That's why I'm transmitting these reflections so abruptly: not to pour oil on the fire, but to help us understand together, once again, that if *we* are the church, we too, first of all, not only have to put in our two-cents' worth, we have to "do" something.... But what should we do?

Make people's attitudes evolve, of course! Stop viewing remarried divorced as people apart; certainly, indeed primarily, rediscover the freedom of Jesus Christ in regard to all systems, rediscover the understanding of the evangelic situations. I would thus gladly plead for an end to the intellectualism, the analyses, the reports and documents that inundate us and that ultimately hide the clear source of the Gospel, the purity of Jesus Christ, and the hope of salvation.

> The Gospel, yes.
> It's time to rediscover:
> the simplicity of its words
> the audacity of its plainness

the power of its radicalism
the insolence of its beatitudes
the provocation of its calls
the clarity of its light
the taste of its salt
the madness of its cross
the utopia of its hope
the breath of its Spirit
the road of love
the truth of joy
the passion of life.

Will we have the courage to be taken at our word by Christ, like all these unhappy people whom Father Congar sees symbolized in Mary Magdalene, in the adulteress, in the publican?

Oh Mary Magdalene
You whom I name
For so many other Mary Magdalenes
Do something up there
If you can
For the unhappy
Who many never know
The embalmed tears
At the feet of him who releases from all sin.

Oh you, adulterous woman
Multitude-woman
Ubiquitous woman
You whose name I don't even know
I've met you
All over the world
The adulterous world
In my adulterous heart
In the hearts of all these adulterous men
Of all these adulterous women
Do something up there
If you can

For all my brothers
Who may never
Know the Word
That forbids us to throw the tiniest stone.

Oh you the publican
I'm not quite sure
That you're not a bit of a Pharisee
But so what, you are what we are
In our disguised poverty
Do something up there
If you can
For the desperate
In the depths of our walled churches
Who may never know
The parable of the saved.

Oh all you canonized sinners
Do something up there
If you can
Ask Jesus the Resurrected
For we hunger
For the thing that you know
And that remains the thing unknown
To so many men:

"Jesus came to save those who are lost."